*Twayne's United States Authors Series*

EDITOR OF THIS VOLUME

Lewis Leary

*University of North Carolina, Chapel Hill*

*Susan and Anna Warner*

TUSAS 312

Susan Warner

Anna Warner

# SUSAN and ANNA WARNER

### By EDWARD HALSEY FOSTER

*Stevens Institute of Technology*

TWAYNE PUBLISHERS

A DIVISION OF G. K. HALL & CO., BOSTON

**Library of Congress Cataloging in Publication Data**

Foster, Edward Halsey.
 Susan and Anna Warner.

 (Twayne's United States authors series ; TUSAS 312)
 Bibliography: p. 129 - 134
 Includes index.
 1. Warner, Susan, 1819 - 1885—Criticism and inter-
pretation. 2. Warner, Anna Bartlett, 1827 - 1915—Criticism and
interpretation. I. Title.
PS3156.F6    831'.03    78-2431
ISBN 0-8057-7232-4

MANUFACTURED IN THE UNITED STATES OF AMERICA

For
John Clark Foster
and
Katherine Hearn Foster

# Contents

# About the Author

Edward Halsey Foster is an associate professor at the Stevens Institute of Technology, where he is the director of the American Studies program. He is the author of several books, including *The Civilized Wilderness* (1975), which is widely regarded as a central work in American Studies. Among his other publications at *Catharine Maria Sedgwick* (1974) in the Twayne United States Authors Series, and, most recently, *Josiah Gregg and Louis Hector Garrard* (1977), a study of the early literature of the American Southwest. He has published numerous articles in American Studies and American literature and has been the recipient of various grants and awards. Professor Foster is married to the former Elaine Dunphy, and they live in New York City and in Cummington, Massachusetts, with their two children.

# *Preface*

Susan and Anna Warner are novelists of much importance to the American literary tradition, but many of their values are so thoroughly different from ours, so clearly a part of an era long past, that critics today find it difficult to evaluate their novels sympathetically. The Warners shared with their original readers various cultural biases and values, which must be understood before the books can be read in the historical context in which they belong. The Warners were didactic novelists: they wrote to teach, and it was, above all, as teachers that they were appreciated by their contemporaries.

My study is concerned largely with the didacticism of the Warners' fiction. It is the aim of this book to make the objectives of this fiction readily understandable to twentieth-century readers. The didactic purposes of the Warners' fiction are outlined, and the historical origins of their social, political, and religious thinking are traced.

In this study, I have tried to show that the Warners' novels are important as, among other things, expressions of the dominant mid-nineteenth-century American culture—the same culture against which writers as different as Melville and Thoreau rebelled. But this book also demonstrates that these novels have a significance beyond their historical value. If one searches nineteenth-century popular fiction for something that has literary value, one searches, by and large, in vain. The nineteenth century judged fiction on the basis of didactic, not literary, value; and, as a result, few of the century's popular works are of serious literary interest. The Warners' novels, especially Susan's, are, however, important forerunners of the "local color" movement that flourished in this country in the mid-nineteenth and early twentieth centuries and are equal, in places, to the very best fiction that this movement produced. Even as demanding a critic as Henry James noted with approval Susan's ability to render concisely and vividly the manners and customs of rural New England.

In the following chapters, the social, religious, and political biases which the Warners shared with their age (or at least with their sympathetic readers) are outlined. In particular, the social and political thinking of their father, Henry Whiting Warner, and the religious thinking of their minister, Thomas Harvey Skinner, are discussed. The Warner sisters, as this book demonstrates, were devoted to the two men, accepted their ideas unconditionally, and incorporated them into *The Wide, Wide World, Queechy, Say and Seal,* and other important novels. I have attempted to show that the first of these novels is designed expressly to teach and illustrate the evangelical Protestant thinking promoted by Skinner, and that the second expresses the patrician, Whig ideals supported by Henry Whiting Warner. Similarly, I have pointed out the nature and origins of the political, social, and religious didacticism in the other important Warner novels, notably *Say and Seal, Dollars and Cents, Wych Hazel, The Gold of Chickaree, Melbourne House, Daisy,* and *Daisy: Second Series.* I have also dealt briefly with the didacticism of several other less well known Warner novels and, in passing, have discussed their religious tracts, books for children, theological works, and other books.

The Warners wrote and edited more than a hundred volumes, but much of this work is of marginal or no literary interest. Susan's works, on the whole, deserve more literary attention than Anna's. Except in those books which she wrote jointly with Susan, Anna's writings are generally weak, the narratives diffuse, and the characterizations vague. Anna is remembered only for a few of her publications, primarily her autobiographical novel *Dollars and Cents,* a few of her hymns, and the novels on which she collaborated with her sister. It was Susan's fiction, not Anna's, that was better known a century ago, and it is Susan's fiction, together with the novels that she wrote jointly with Anna, that deserves our special attention today.

I have also dealt with Susan's attitude toward women in her fiction; and this is important in order to correct the mistaken but common view of her as an early feminist. In fact, her attitude toward women appears to have been rather conventional; her books provide idealized images of domesticity and, using biblical references as support, suggest that wives must learn to submit themselves to their husbands—surely no feminist doctrine, although one that was common in the mid-nineteenth century.

Considerable attention is given in this study to the importance of

the Warners' novels in the development of the local color movement in American literature, and the use of regional customs and
dialect, particularly in *The Wide, Wide World, Queechy*, and *Say
and Seal* is documented. The Warner books are important among
the few surviving records of a once flourishing but now vanished
rural American culture—the backwoods Yankee world that existed
in the first half of the nineteenth century. This introduction and
many of the chapters that follow were written on an upland Yankee
farm from which I can look across to Lebanon Mountain where a
portion of *The Wide, Wide World* is set. The landscape in front of
me is very much like that which the Warners saw a century ago, but
the Yankees and the culture that once thrived here have long since
vanished. The landscape remains, but the culture survives only in
letters, essays, stories, and, above all, novels, among which the
Warners' deserve particular attention.

Finally, I should note that at many points, this study makes considerable use of biographical data, for the Warners, unlike such contemporaries as Hawthorne and Poe, made extensive use of their own
lives in their fiction. All of the Warners' major works are, at least in
part, records of their own experiences, especially in New England
villages. One positive result is many of their novels contain detailed
records of the manners, customs, and dialects they encountered. A
person interested in the life and culture of rural New England
would do well to seek out in second-hand bookstores and rare book
collections copies of those Warner novels which, although now
forgotten, were apparently once known to the vast majority of
readers in America.

EDWARD HALSEY FOSTER

*Cummington, Massachusetts, and New York City*

# Acknowledgments

My study of the Warners would not have been possible without the help of various scholars who freely offered important suggestions and criticism, and of librarians, who opened to me collections of manuscripts and rare books that proved invaluable to my purpose. Among the individuals and institutions to whom I am indebted are the Constitution Island Association and its president, Mrs. Genevieve H. Lewis; the New-York Historical Society; the New York Public Library; the Boston Public Library; the Special Collections of the Columbia University Library; Miss Roxanne Young and the staff of the Long Island Historical Society; the Presbyterian Historical Society; Union Theological Seminary; Mrs. Dorothy Hucke of the First Presbyterian Church in New York; the interlibrary loan department of the library at the Stevens Institute of Technology; Mrs. Eleanor Shea and the staff of Forbes Library (Northampton, Mass.); the Old Bookshop in Northampton; and the library at Union College. I am also indebted to numerous public officials in New York who tracked down public documents concerning the Warners with a thoroughness and efficiency that would put many seasoned scholars to shame.

Mr. William Lewis graciously took me on a tour of his home and grounds—the former Warner homestead in Canaan, N.Y. For other good services, I am indebted to Leonard Ellis, Mara Lusis, and Mabel Baker, official historian of the Constitution Island Association. The Reverend David Warren of the West End Presbyterian Church tracked down several biblical references for me and helped at other points. For the general knowledge of the religious context in which the Warner books were written, I have a long-standing debt—one which should have been repaid many years ago—to Mrs. Leslie G. Derosia. Katherine and John, the scholars-in-training to whom this book is dedicated, accompanied me through endless stacks, card catalogs, and reels of microfilm.

Finally I am indebted to Mr. Orson Henry and the deacons of the Williamsburg (Mass.) Congregational Church, who several years

*Acknowledgments*

ago let me and my family spend the summer in their huge Victorian parsonage. It was in the library here that I first read *The Wide, Wide World*. A more appropriate setting could not, I think, have been found.

# Chronology

| | |
|---|---|
| 1860 | Susan and Anna published *Say and Seal*. |
| 1860s | Robert Carter became Susan's major publisher. |
| 1868 | Susan published *Daisy* and *Daisy: Second Series*. |
| 1875 | Henry Whiting Warner died. |
| 1877 | Susan published her "factual" novels. |
| 1885 | |
| 1885 | Susan died March 17. Secretary of War granted permission for her to be buried in the cemetery at West Point. Frances Warner ("Aunt Fanny") died October 31. |
| 1908 | Anna sold Constitution Island for $150,000 with the provisions that she retain life tenancy and that the island eventually be given to the United States. |
| 1909 | Anna published her final work, a biography of Susan. |
| 1915 | Anna died January 22. Buried beside her sister in the cemetery at West Point. |
| 1916 | Martelaer's Rock Association formed in part to preserve the Warner house on Constitution Island. |
| 1925 | Name of Martelaer's Rock Association changed to its present name, Constitution Island Association. *Letters and Memories of Susan and Anna Bartlett Warner* by Olivia Egleston Phelps Stokes published. |
| 1946 | Historical marker honoring Susan and Anna erected at the Warner homestead in Canaan, New York. |

CHAPTER 1

# Fashion and Famine

W E go in and come out, and the effect rather is that we have
nothing to do with the world. Every human tie, out of our quartette,
is so broken and fastened off. . . . Five years ago, and we were hardly left
at home two or three evenings in a month. . . , and now nobody almost is
anything to us.
                        —Susan Warner, journal entry, December 15, 1850[1]

### I   Gathering at the River

Among the traditions at West Point a century ago was the weekly
Bible-meeting held by two spinsters for young cadets. During the
week, the cadets studied mathematics, engineering, and military
history; but on warm Sunday afternoons, a select group (many more
wanted to go than could be accommodated) was rowed across the
Hudson to the island where the spinsters lived. The two women
were sisters and lived with their elderly father and his sister in an
old farmhouse. All four were intensely religious and no doubt concerned with the cadets' religious life—or rather lack of it. And the
Bible-meetings more than made up for any lack.

After arriving at the island, the cadets were grouped around the
older sister, correctly dressed in a fashion that had once been popular but that was now merely peculiar or affected. She led the
cadets in hymn-singing, then lectured on the Bible for a half hour or
more. The younger sister then served her guests light refreshments;
and later in the afternoon, the cadets were rowed back to the
academy.

Some of the cadets who attended these meetings were probably
less interested in hymns and the Bible than in meeting these sisters,
whose exaggeratedly gracious manners and eccentric dress had long
made them notable (or notorious) at the academy and in the surrounding villages. Their ingratiating manners and sheer persistence
had made their Bible-meetings a tradition of cadet life, and there

17

were surely few cadets who could not recognize the sisters at sight. But the sisters, as everyone at the academy knew, were famous far beyond West Point—and for reasons very different from Bible-meetings. The older woman was Susan Warner, whose novel *The Wide, Wide World* (1850) had been one of the most popular books ever published; and her sister Anna was a well-known author of novels and children's books.

It is unlikely that many West Point cadets read the Warners' books, for these sentimental tales of domestic and religious crises offered little to interest men. On the other hand, surely many of their mothers and sisters had shed tears over the misfortunes of Ellen Montgomery in *The Wide, Wide World* and of Fleda Ringgan in *Queechy* (1852), or had wept their way through the domestic distress and miseries of Anna Warner's best seller, *Dollars and Cents* (1852).

The Warners' novels were written for women. They dealt primarily with religious and moral issues; and because of this, their fiction was altogether welcome in their time, permeated as it was by evangelical piety and refined moral standards. Not less important to their popularity was their firmly Protestant stand on moral and religious issues. Henry James, writing in *The Nation* in 1865, acknowledged that all his readers were Protestants.[2] In the 1850s and 1860s, when the Warners' novels attained their greatest popularity, their religious sentiments reflected a largely national, not merely sectarian, temper.

These novels, particularly Susan Warner's, utilized much American local color and regional detail; and it is in fact the acute and fully realized sense of time and place in the best of the novels that makes them interesting to the literary critic and historian today. Although the Warners were, first of all, concerned with moral and religious issues, they were also interested in the details of regional social customs and dialects; and Susan Warner, though not her sister, recorded them with a precision matched by few of the more famous local colorists—Sarah Orne Jewett, Mary E. Wilkins Freeman, and Alice Brown—who published their books later in the century. The details of local color that interested the Warners were, however, almost solely those of social and domestic life—worlds inhabited largely by women. What happened in the kitchen was of far greater interest to the Warners and their readers than what happened in the office.

The Warner sisters were indeed seldom interested in men—in either life or fiction—unless, like the cadets who came for Bible-meetings, they were in need of religious or moral improvement. This is not to say that the sisters were feminists—which they decidedly were not—or that they disliked or distrusted men. Quite simply, the Warners, like their female readership, had little knowledge of, and even less interest in, traditional male occupations and customs. The realm of womanly activities and responsibilities was large and well defined, and in it the sisters found sufficient materials not only for rewarding and purposeful lives but also for several of the most popular and influential novels of the day.

## II   *Young Ladies of Fashion*

All of the Warners' best-known novels are in part transcriptions of their own experiences and family memories, so that it is important to know something, if only in outline, of their lives. *The Wide, Wide World, Queechy,* and *Dollars and Cents* concern wealthy, fashionable individuals and families who are reduced to poverty. It was a social and economic fall that the sisters knew well; at the time the first of these books was published, the Warners were virtually bankrupt, and yet they had been, a short while before, among the richest and most respected families in New York society. There are close parallels between the Warners' lives and their fiction, and no one doubts that the first inspired the second. However, the best of their books are never *merely* autobiographical. The Warners successfully transformed their experiences into works of fiction that have far more than autobiographical or historical interest.

The social and economic comforts that the sisters knew as children were largely the result of their father's ambitions and achievements. Although their grandfather had prospered and served in the state legislature, the family was of little note or influence. Their father, Henry Whiting Warner, was descended from New England farmers, but he was far more ambitious than any of his ancestors, and, after preparing for college at Lenox Academy in Massachusetts, spent four years at Union College, then went to New York and studied law in the office of Robert Emmet. Warner had literary ambitions as well and wrote several books of political as well as literary interest. His major occupations were, however, law and real estate; and in both, he was enormously successful. As a result, his social rise was rapid; undoubtedly a brilliant man and a good conversationalist, he was soon welcome at the homes of the best families in New York.

In 1810, when Henry Warner arrived in New York, the city's most fashionable address was Hudson Square, four blocks of brick townhouses surrounding a small landscaped park to which only residents and their guests were admitted.[3] Fittingly for one as ambitious as he, it was in one of the homes here that he met his future wife, Anna Marsh Bartlett, a woman with social credentials much superior to his, who had spent her childhood in Newport, Providence, New York, and Jamaica, Long Island, where her stepfather had a large country estate. Her father, Isaac Bartlett, died when she was a child, but her mother soon remarried. The stepfather was Cornelius I. Bogert, a New York lawyer of some importance and much wealth who traced his lineage back to the city's original Dutch founders. Among his friends were Rufus King, Samuel Ward, and other political and financial leaders of the day. His stepdaughter was brought up with all the comforts and luxuries available to a young lady of fashion.

Anna Bartlett and Henry Warner were married in 1817 at the Episcopal Church near the Bogert estate. They were soon counted among the prosperous young couples in New York. Their daughter Susan was born two years later; Anna, in 1827. (Two other daughters and a son died in infancy.) Henry Warner had every reason to congratulate himself: born on an upland New England farm, he had become one of New York's most promising lawyers and respected citizens. There was a social and economic chasm between the two worlds—a fact that his daughters later documented with considerable detail in their fiction.

In 1822, he moved his family to a small country farm on Gowanus Lane near what was then the small village of Brooklyn, from which he travelled by ferry to his law offices in lower Manhattan. Winters were spent in New York. Many years later, Anna used her memories of winters in the city and summers at the little house on Gowanus Lane as literary material in *Mr. Rutherford's Children*. It was an idyllic childhood, unbroken until the spring of 1828, when Mrs. Warner died. Her duties as homemaker were assumed by Henry Warner's sister Frances, or "Aunt Fanny" as she was known to the children; and the quiet summers in the country, alternating with winters in New York, continued unbroken until the early 1830s. By this time, Warner's legal work and investments had prospered enormously, and he moved his family to a townhouse in Manhattan at 461 Broome Street near Broadway.[4]

Many New York fortunes like Warner's were made in these years. The success of the Erie Canal, completed in 1825, made New York the nation's leading port. The city soon doubled, then tripled in population. Fortunes, especially in real estate, were made overnight. The site of 461 Broome Street had been open country a few years earlier; in the 1830s it was in the midst of a densely settled and rapidly expanding city. Broome Street was at this time a fashionable address—incredible though this may seem to anyone who knows that run-down area today—but it was by no means as fashionable as the Warners' next address, St. Mark's Place, to which they moved in 1835 and where they remained until financial difficulties forced them to sell their property in 1838.[5] These years also saw the purchase of Constitution Island across the Hudson from the United States Military Academy at West Point. Henry Warner purchased the property at the urging of his brother Thomas, chaplain at the academy, with the hope that it would prove not only a wise financial investment but also a suitable location for his family's country estate.[6] Had all gone as planned, the Warners would have enjoyed as elegant and fashionable a life as anyone in America at that time. If their father had not suffered financial losses in the Panic of 1837 and the years that followed, Susan and Anna would surely have married into other established New York families and would have lived enviably comfortable and elegant lives.

Henry Warner's losses in 1837 and 1838 were enormous, and the mansion on St. Mark's Place had to be sold. Summers could be spent at Constitution Island, but during the winters, there was enough money to rent only a few rooms in the city. In 1842, Warner could not afford even meager quarters like these, and the family spent the winter in the cold, drafty farmhouse on the island. When Henry Warner purchased the island, he had looked on the old house there as merely a temporary residence, but in the end it became his home and his daughters' for the rest of their lives. Anna was still living here when she died eighty years later.[7]

### III  *Conversion*

Shortly after the Warners' economic difficulties began, Susan, walking along Waverly Place in New York, encountered a woman who was among the leaders of fashionable society, "and as they

passed," wrote Anna many years later, "this woman's brow was so
slight and cool, that it almost had the air of a rebuff. Whether so
meant or not does not matter; it seemed so to my sister. And as she
walked on, with that sense of check so painful to a young person, all
her nerves astir at the supposed slight, she said in her heart that she
would put her happiness in a safer place, beyond the reach of scorn-
ful fingers. She would have something that should stand, though
the whole world went to pieces."[8] That "safer place" was, of course,
to be found in religion; and through evangelicalism, the dominant
Protestant movement of the day, Susan gained a comprehensive
sense of personal worth that seemed to compensate for whatever she
had lost in the family's fall from social grace.

In 1836, at the peak of his prosperity, Henry Warner purchased a
pew in the newly established Mercer Street Presbyterian Church
near his home on St. Mark's Place. The minister was Thomas
Harvey Skinner, a former professor of sacred rhetoric at the An-
dover Theological Seminary. One of the most influential and
respected theologians of his day, Skinner's particular theological interest was sacred rhetoric, and he eventually left the Mercer Street
Church so that he could accept an appointment at New York's
Union Theological Seminary, of which he was a founder. From the
accounts that have come down to us, he seems to have been an extremely learned and highly respected gentleman; certainly the
Warner sisters held him in highest regard, and the theology that he
preached profoundly influenced their fiction.

To the sisters, Skinner was a man of enormous significance: "So
grave, so loving, so wise, so tender," remembered Anna, "and with
that wonderful smile coming out now and then. The holy face, the
gentle bend of the head at the answer to some question. . . ."[9] No
person, except their father, was more highly respected by them. On
April 2, 1841, they became members of Skinner's church; it was
clearly the most important moment in their lives.

Susan and Anna literally devoted themselves to their religion and
to their church. Their writings, too, were part of this devotion; all
were aimed at theological ends. Clearly the sisters' new importance
in their church provided a psychological compensation for their loss
of social prestige, but to say this is not to question the sincerity of
their religious commitment. No one can read their religious novels,
tracts, and essays without a sense that their religious convictions
were both intense and profound.

As children, Susan and Anna had spent little time together. Susan was eight years the senior, and when she became a young lady she spent much time visiting and attending social gatherings, while Anna was left at home in the care of Aunt Fanny or the servants. Mutual interests in church matters finally brought the sisters together, and from that moment until Susan's death more than forty years later, they were seldom apart. "The bond which was knit between us two," wrote Anna many years after her sister's death, "should outlast all time and change. For still I find myself questioning what she would have me do; still, unconsciously, I say 'we,' and 'ours.' And if I write on the fly leaf of a book, it is often the two names together, as they used to be. Only when some sharp earthly wind smites me in the face, then I cry out for joy, that it cannot reach her."[10]

### IV   *Fame without Fortune*

Susan Warner's first two novels, *The Wide, Wide World* (1850) and *Queechy* (1852), and Anna's *Dollars and Cents* (1852) were immediately and enormously popular among both general readers and critics. None of their later books were as popular as these, but, from time to time, they published novels that received good notices and sales; and all of them remained in print for many years. If the large number of copies available today through secondhand book dealers are any indication, some of the later novels had large print runs and were best sellers. *Say and Seal* (1860), *Wych Hazel* (1876), and *The Gold of Chickaree* (1876)—all of which the sisters wrote jointly—may have sold well also both here and abroad; but lack of adequate data—nineteenth-century publishers' and booksellers' sales figures are notoriously incomplete and, at times, inaccurate—prevent us from knowing exactly how popular they were. Whatever the case, the sisters' writings provided their family's sole income. They always had a book or two in progress, and sometimes the rights to a book were sold before it was finished or in print. Money was always needed, and the family could not wait for royalties.

In the early 1850s, Henry Warner tried to reestablish himself as a lawyer in New York, but he was an old man by then, and his friends from prosperous days were either retired or dead. He could not find enough legal work to support his family, and his assets, which had been invested in real estate, had long since gone to pay debts.

His daughters literally *had* to write; it was the only way to avoid complete bankruptcy. Each morning before dawn, they were up, had completed breakfast, and were busily writing. Tracts, Bible studies, essays, stories, children's books, and novels—more than a hundred volumes were written and published; but since the sisters sold their interest in some of their more popular books outright rather than wait for royalties, they were seldom truly well off. When any income could be spared, their father invested it; and, from time to time, these investments were fairly lucrative. But the returns were never sufficient to support the family, and so another book was always in progress. Susan Warner was working on another novel at the time of her death in 1885, and Anna went on to write many more books, the last of which, a biography of her sister, appeared in 1909. A year earlier she had sold Constitution Island, although retaining life tenancy, to Mrs. Russell Sage for a substantial sum; and so in her last years—she died in 1915—she was able to enjoy the sort of financial comfort that no one in her family had known since the beginning of their economic troubles more than seventy years before.

## V  *Church and State*

Without exception, the Warners' novels are explicitly didactic, and the religious and social standards that they illustrate and teach are those of an upper-class, urban gentry. Socially and politically, the sisters' sympathies were democratic but not egalitarian. The novels also express the dominant evangelical Protestant theology of the day as modified by an essentially urban and conservative temperament. *The Wide, Wide World* and its successors can be adequately evaluated only within the frames of nineteenth-century social and religious thought. The critic who does not understand the novels' social and religious assumptions can easily misinterpret or misjudge the sisters' literary and didactic objectives.

*Queechy* more than any other novel by the Warners is concerned with manners and with the social and moral distinctions that they imply. The enormous significance of manners to the social and religious nature of the Warners' world will be discussed in Chapter 3; but it is worth noting here that all of their fiction, although directly involved with other didactic matters, is necessarily also concerned with manners. The theological and social values that the novels teach were not merely abstract or theoretical matters. A man's values were reflected in his behavior and were, therefore, matters of immediate and practical social consequence. The Warners took from the Protestant elite, that upper-class, urban gentry to which they belonged, not only their social and religious values but also the manners with which to dramatize them.

Long after the Warners had been forgotten by their friends in the prosperous days at St. Mark's Place, they continued to think of themselves as members of the social elite—and not without some reason, since that elite identified itself essentially with a shared code of manners rather than wealth. The Warners' economic losses in no way tempered their social and political attitudes. Significantly, Henry Whiting Warner in 1838—an economically disastrous year for him—published a conservative, anti-Jacksonian study of American government, *An Inquiry Into the Moral and Religious Character of the American Government.* To be sure, the book was begun during a more prosperous year, but since he neither revised the book nor withdrew it from publication, there is no reason to assume that his political and social theories were affected by his financial failures. Above all, he continued to uphold the patrician's attitude toward society. Shortly after he failed to reestablish a law practice, he published a second, equally conservative treatise, *The Liberties of America* (1853). Once again, economic and professional failure did not cause him to reverse or, indeed, temper his social and political attitudes.

*The Liberties of America*—which he called "a pioneer effort" in "a *literature of freedom*"—argued that liberty was socially and personally viable only within certain restraints—economic, legal, and moral—which he proceeded to list and describe.[11] "Liberty," he concluded, "is an *effect*, not an independent essence; *a result of political order. . . .*"[12] There is, of course, nothing unique in the argument; it was in fact the very basis of American patrician dogma. In effect, as men like Warner believed, the frontier tried to evade political authority, while the patrician East insisted on, and found new ways to justify, social and political control. One imagines Henry Whiting Warner, secure on St. Mark's Place, shocked by what he heard of President Andrew Jackson's apparent egalitarianism. And the specter of egalitarianism continued to reappear and was deeply frightening to anyone with his patrician bias. In turn, his daughters' novels, like his books, offer a deeply conservative, patrician view of social order and hierarchy. In the conflict between public law and personal freedom, both he and his daughters chose law: social and political authority must be used to keep personal behavior in check.

The patrician view reinforced and was reinforced by the dominant Protestant theology of the time, evangelicalism; the connection between the two is explicit in *An Inquiry Into the Moral and Religious Character of the American Government*. Warner wrote the book at a time when the patrician East was still politically disorganized. The patricians eventually found their answer to the Jacksonians and regained political authority through the Whig Party, but this was by no means evident or predictable in the mid-1830s when Warner began writing his *Inquiry*. The Whigs were organized in 1834, but not until 1840 did they have sufficient national authority to capture the presidency and rout the Jacksonians.

Warner and the Whigs split with the Jacksonians specifically over the issue of the separation of church and state. In 1832, President Jackson, noting that the two institutions should remain separate, refused to appoint a day of national humiliation. At issue was a cholera epidemic in Europe, and many feared that it would eventually reach America—as, in fact, it did. A day of national humiliation would presumably have appeased the Deity and kept the epidemic from the American shore, but Jackson refused to act. In the ensuing national dismay, Jackson's enemies discovered support for their cause. Jackson also insisted that postal service not be halted for the Sabbath—much to the horror of religious Americans. One can be sure that Warner was among the most incredulous and shocked, since his Sabbaths were entirely devoted to religious matters.[13] His *Inquiry*—which he published anonymously and which has from time to time been misattributed to Theodore Frelinghuysen—is a classic statement of the Whig's position.

Warner argued that church and state must institutionally be kept separate. A generation earlier, he might have argued otherwise, but in 1838, the argument would have been pointless. There were, for one thing, no officially sanctioned churches left by this time. The last had been the Congregational Church, which lost its official role in Massachusetts in 1833. But while there was no institutional link between church and state, the state's moral character, insisted Warner, should obey the dictates of Christianity. The *Inquiry* expresses a clear horror of Jacksonianism and argues the Whig's religious position with an intense, strident, evangelical fervor.

"Christianity," Warner concluded, ". . . is a supporter of the laws. Need this be proved? And what is liberty but the certainty, the impartiality, the sovereignty, of the laws, as contradistinguished from the will of man?"[14] The argument was essentially that of *The Liberties of America*, fifteen years later: the individual will cannot be trusted; it must be subjected to a higher authority.

The Whig message was not lost on the Warner sisters. In their last books, they were still fighting the anti-Jacksonian cause—a cause which the rest of the country had long forgotten. The Warners lost their social and economic position at the precise moment that Whig enthusiasm was reaching its height. Excluded from new political and social circles, the Warners did not realize that the old cause had long been replaced by other issues. In a sense, the sisters were like their father, politically and socially frozen in the era of Whig ascendancy.

## VI *The Theology of Mercer Street*

The religious base from which the Warners derived their social and political theories was evangelicalism, particularly the variety preached by the "New School" Presbyterians. The academic center of "New School" thought was Union Theological Seminary, then located on University Place, a few blocks from the mansion on St. Mark's Place and close to the rented rooms which the Warners later occupied. One of the leaders of the "New School" and a founder of the seminary was the Warners' minister, Thomas Harvey Skinner.

Skinner, his biographer claimed, believed that the division between the "Old School" and "New School" was not profound and lay merely in differences over "the best modes of viewing, stating and explaining certain of [the Bible's] dogmatic truths."[15] These are the words, however, of a theologian who wished to heal the breach that had fractured his church. In fact, the division was profound, as Skinner well knew, and was never actually resolved, merely forgotten with the passing of the "Old School."

One of Skinner's closest friends was the Reverend Albert Barnes, a fellow classmate at the Princeton Seminary. In 1831, Barnes was charged with heresy by the General Assembly of the Presbyterian Church for his frankly unorthodox attitude toward basic principles of Presbyterianism, summarized in the Westminster Confession. Two years later, another friend, Edward Beecher, was also tried for heresy. Both Beecher and Barnes as well as others against whom the charge of heresy was leveled, were acquitted, but the heresy charges soon precipitated a schism in the church.

The "Old School" conservatives, who, ironically, were centered at Princeton, the very seminary at which Barnes and Skinner had been educated, were repelled by the excessive emotional character of revivalism and insisted on a strict, doctrinaire, systematic theology. Both schools were fundamentally revivalistic, but while the "New School" was more concerned with conversion and faith, the "Old School" emphasized doctrine and the sacraments. In effect, the "Old School" insisted on a strict adherence to traditional doctrine, while the "New School" was willing to adapt or revise doctrine when it seemed appropriate for revivalistic ends. The "New School" identified a convert by his faith: the "Old School," by his acceptance and understanding of the Westminster Confession.

The acrimony between the two schools was at its height between 1835 and 1844—the years which saw the establishment of the Mercer Street Church, the publication of Warner's *Inquiry*, and his daughters' religious conversion. The Warners were surely aware of the theological split within their church, and that schism or at least the "New School" argument was ultimately central to the Warners' novels.

When Susan and Anna Warner joined the Mercer Street Church, they were not put through a rigorous cross-examination on the Westminster Confession and the fine points of church doctrine. Rather, Skinner and one of the church elders asked general questions about the nature of the sisters' beliefs and religious affections. It was a theological approach that Skinner and Edward Beecher had discussed in a textbook of revivalism, *Hints, Designed to Aid Christians in Their Efforts to Convert Men to God* (1832): "by all means avoid making the impression on the minds of those with whom you converse, that the work of becoming religious requires a considerable time to be spent in protracted efforts."[16] Religious conversion depended simply on "an intelligent, voluntary, indivisible act of the mind, in which it ceases to rebel against God, submits to his authority, and accepts of his mercy."[17] Personally, Skinner was a Calvinist, and he subscribed fully to the tenets of the Westminster Confession, but he was far more interested in faith than orthodoxy as evidence of conversion. In turn, the Warner novels preach faith, not orthodoxy, as the principal indication that a person is on the route to salvation.

In his *Religion of the Bible* (1838), Skinner amplified his views. He could not be satisfied simply with a religion that amounted to little but show or ritual, nor could he be satisfied with one characterized solely by obedience to doctrine and biblical demands. Ritual and doctrine had their value, but what he desired was a *"Spiritual Religion"*—a religion, that is,

which can be satisfied with nothing merely external, however blameless and fair. The offering up of prayer and praise, meditation on the Scriptures, attendance upon ordinances, liberality toward the poor, the utmost exactness and irreproachableness of life—these do not meet its demands, unless there is correspondent sensibility and life in the heart. There must be a feeling of the Divine presence; a relishing of the Divine excellence; a heart-assured persuasion of the Divine favour and complacency. God must be enjoyed; or there will be disquietude of soul. . . .[18]

What Skinner calls "Spiritual Religion" is what is more widely known as evangelicalism. Religion in this instance is seen as a matter of the "heart"—in effect, a matter of emotions or sensibility. Some evangelicals believed that religious sensibility was not emotional; but others, the most famous of whom was the great revivalist Charles Grandison Finney, disagreed. In any case, the evangelicals all believed that religion was basically not an intellectual concern—an assertion which, because of its very popularity, was profoundly disconcerting to the advocates of the old systematic, intellectually structured theologies. According to Skinner's *Religion of the Bible,*

[Christ] has no deep theory, no subtle discriminations, no elaborate reasoning; but makes his appeals to man's common sense, and makes them in such a manner, that common sense in a child, can neither misapprehend nor resist them. Let it not be again said, that the subject is mysterious. If there be mystery here, it is not the mystery of the subject, but of a perverse and unteachable heart.[19]

Christ's message was said to be not a complex matter which only the learned theologian could fully understand, but rather something immediately knowable to all. The message was clearly diagramed in the Bible and easily recognized by the "heart." The Christian's business was to study the Bible, understand divine purpose, and freely submit his own will to it.

Skinner's theology—like the political and social theories of Henry

Whiting Warner—was exceptionally conservative, and he was clearly distrustful of human nature. Both Warner and Skinner felt the need for a complete submission to higher authority; the individual and society had to be guided by divine purpose; this purpose should be immediately apprehended by the Christian, and his failure to do so could only be disastrous. In the social and political realms, that failure, Warner believed, would lead to chaos. According to Skinner and Beecher in their book on revivalism, those who did not apprehend that purpose or who did not follow it were "as really and fearfully exposed to eternal perdition, as men in a burning house are to perish by the flames. If you saw any of your friends or neighbors in such peril," they asked their readers, "would it need peculiar qualifications to lift up the voice of warning, and bid them escape for their lives, or to rush in and save them with fear, pulling them out of the fire? And can you not with equal, nay, greater earnestness, warn sinners to flee from the wrath to come; and if they linger, lay hold on them, being merciful unto them, and with irresistable persuasions, induce them, without delay, to seek safety in the city of refuge? Make, then, no more excuses for neglect of so plain a duty; the claims of God are upon you; the cries of perishing souls come up around you; the groans of a dying world are sounding in your ears, and can you remain longer inactive? Break, then, the bands of sloth; engage at once in the work; be courageous; be wise; turn many to righteousness, and you shall shine as the brightness of the firmament, and as the stars, for ever and ever."[20]

## VII   Church Work

The authoritarianism, the self-righteousness, and the anti-intellectualism of "New School" Presbyterian evangelicalism had a great appeal for self-made New York merchants and businessmen. For the most part, they lacked formal education, and their practical natures generally distrusted learning. They also distrusted the opinion of the general populace—a distrust that they shared generally with anti-Jacksonians and specifically with well-educated professionals like Henry Warner. The Mercer Street Church provided a spiritual home for the new merchant aristocracy; with a congregation of undoubted piety, decided wealth, and good social credentials, it was an ideal church, in a sense, for the Warners, clinging to the remnants of their former social prestige.

All of the Warners and especially the sisters immersed themselves in church activities. Sundays began with Sunday school and Bible classes, followed by the regular morning service. In the afternoon, the Sunday school met again, and there was another church service, which was followed in the evening by a prayer meeting. Every Tuesday evening as well as the first Monday of the month, there was another prayer meeting; and on Thursdays, there was a lecture at the church. "We never thought of accepting any other invitation on Church nights," Anna wrote, "and apart from the duty, the going was always a joy."[21] Their time was also occupied in distributing tracts; attending church sewing societies; collecting, door to door, for missions; and above all, trying to convert others to the evangelical persuasion.

Time was divided between, on the one hand, their home and their father and, on the other, the church and Dr. Skinner. The sisters heroized both men, saw them only in ideal terms. "If I could only see things as Dr. Skinner sees them!" Susan told her sister. "What beauty and glory, to *his* eye, beam from passages where I never was struck with anything particularly. It is a happiness to know at any rate that the source of his light is open to me too."[22] Inevitably, the Warners' novels express the political and religious thinking of their father and their minister; and in this fact lies one explanation for the great popularity of their earliest books. When *The Wide, Wide World, Queechy,* and *Dollars and Cents* were published, the Whigs and their philosophy were politically in power; and evangelical Christianity had become the dominant religious idiom in America.

## VIII  *The Domestic Novel*

In their novels, the Warners tried to make the various religious, social, and political theories we have examined applicable to women's lives. As noted earlier, these novels have little to do with the business and professional worlds of men; the typical setting for one of the Warners' novels is the home, and the principal characters, with few exceptions, are women. Some of the novels —*Queechy* in particular—describe in considerable detail the household duties of women. If typically male activities are mentioned at all, they are mentioned briefly and only in passing.

As students of American social and cultural history know, domesticity was idealized by the nineteenth century and viewed largely as the source of the country's moral and religious strength.[23]

The popular annuals—books often given to friends as Christmas presents—invariably contained sentimental poems, sketches, stories, and engravings of domestic life. Their titles included "My Sister," "To My Mother," "My Mother's Bible," even "The Birthplace of Washington."[24] "The day is not distant," wrote the author of the last of these, "when the votaries of enlightened freedom, throughout the enfranchised world, will make their pilgrimages to this cradle of its great apostle, with a fervor infinitely more exalted than ever thrilled the followers of the Prophet."[25] It was, of course, Mount Vernon, rather than Washington's birthplace, that eventually became a national shrine—but the underlying issue remained: a man's most sacred associations were with his home. The idealization of domesticity was ultimately defended by a theologian as influential and respected as Horace Bushnell, and Catharine Beecher in a series of treatises on domesticity elevated the subject virtually to the level of a science.[26]

The Warner novels were an important contribution to the era's conception of ideal domesticity. They suggested that it was a woman's duty to conduct not only her life but also her household according to ideal moral and social principles. This was the common message of Bushnell, Beecher, and other American writers on domesticity, but none reached an audience as huge as the Warners'. It is obviously impossible to document quantitatively any relationship between the popularity of the Warners' novels and the increasing idealization of domesticity that permeated their era; but the wide audience that those novels reached suggests, at the least, that their influence was far from negligible.

## IX    New England and New York

The Warners' novels, particularly Susan's, have a continuing literary value because their didacticism, unlike the didacticism of most other domestic and sentimental novels of the time, is grounded in realistic images of life in rural New England and upper-class New York. It would be a mistake to argue that either of the Warners was interested in these images for their intrinsic interest. Such images were generally important only when they could be used to illustrate didactic points or in other ways contribute to didactic purposes. In this respect, the Warners were very different from later "local colorists." In the Warners' novels, there is little cultural objectivity, few attempts to view a culture objectively or comprehensively. Local color in the Warners' novels is seldom more than a fictive convenience, yet the realism and local color—whatever their didactic purpose—give such books as *The Wide, Wide World* decided literary importance, a fact that we will later discuss and that has been recognized by critics ever since Henry James called attention to it more than a century ago.[27]

Because local color was, for the Warners, merely a means to an end, they could as easily and, they apparently thought, successfully write novels based on their readings as they could write novels based on their experiences. The sisters wrote many books with settings based solely on travel books, novels, and stereopticon views. What they sought was fictional substance to illustrate the ideas and values that they taught. In fact, the novels based on secondary sources seem today highly stylized and forced; the diction, flat; and the descriptions, schematic and conventional. The Warners' best novels are uniformly those that draw on their personal experiences.

Olivia Stokes, whose reminiscences of the Warner sisters were published in 1925, called their novels "stories, for I recall Miss Anna's look of what seemed to me troubled surprise when I once spoke of them as Miss Susan's novels. In her younger days many persons holding strict ideas kept aloof from novels."[28] The anecdote is significant: the Warners were novelists virtually in spite of themselves. Some critics have pointed out the apparent incongruity at the end of *The Wide, Wide World* when the hero makes the heroine promise never to read a novel, but the incongruity would have passed unnoticed by the author and her religious audience. *The Wide, Wide World* was written for theological, not aesthetic or literary, ends; and it was as a theological work that it was originally judged. Nothing would have astonished or, one imagines, disconcerted the sisters more than to find critics discussing their novels as literature and listing them, as they have often been listed, among the earliest works of local color and American literary Realism.

### CHAPTER 2

# The Perils of Apostasy

*[The Wide, Wide World]* was written in closest reliance upon God: for thoughts, for power, and for words. Not the mere vague wish to write a book that should do service to her Master: but a vivid, constant, looking to him for guidance and help [sic]: the worker and her work both laid humbly at the Lord's feet.

—Anna Warner, *Susan Warner*[1]

## I  *A Book That Would Sell*

Susan and Anna Warner spent most of their lives from 1838 until their deaths many decades later, in the old farmhouse, "Wood-crags," on Constitution Island. It was here that most of their books were written. The first was begun in the winter of 1847 - 48. Anna wrote it as part of a children's game, *Robinson Crusoe's Farmyard*, which she had devised to teach natural history to children. The game included twenty-four hand-painted cards with pictures of animals, and the accompanying book described the animals and gave answers to questions printed on the backs of the cards. The publisher was George P. Putnam, who was later to make a fortune by publishing *The Wide, Wide World* and *Queechy*.

*Robinson Crusoe's Farmyard* provided the Warners, who were nearly destitute, with greatly needed funds, yet if the family was to survive, it would be necessary, they knew, to find other sources of income. One evening during the winter when Anna was writing her book, Aunt Fanny, turning to Susan, remarked, "I believe if you would try, you could write a story." As Anna later wrote, her aunt had meant a story "That would sell"—a means of lifting the family out of poverty.[2] Anna believed that her sister began *The Wide, Wide World* that evening. It was completed a year and a half later but, at first, was not offered to any publisher. When the book finally was offered to publishers, the results were discouraging. Virtually every major publisher refused it. The reader at Harper's scribbled "Fudge!" on one of the pages, and at Carters, which later became one of the Warners' major publishers, no one bothered to read the manuscript. Finally it was taken to George P. Putnam, who did not read it himself but asked his mother, who was visiting him at the time, for her opinion. "If you never publish another book," Mrs. Putnam said, "publish this!"[3] But Putnam remained unconvinced, and although, at his mother's urging, he agreed to publish it, he decided to print only 750 copies.

*The Wide, Wide World* was issued in December, 1850. To Putnam's considerable surprise, it received extraordinarily favorable reviews, one of which concluded that the author had "few equals, and no superiors, on either side of the Atlantic," while another claimed that the book was "capable of doing more good than any other work, other than the Bible."[4] The first edition sold out quickly, and Putnam, still cautious and a little incredulous, issued a second of 750 copies. This, too, sold out quickly, and a third edition of 750 or 1,000 copies was proposed. By the end of 1852, the book was heading toward its fourteenth edition and its reputation as one of the greatest publishing successes of all time. With the sole exception of *Uncle Tom's Cabin*, it was the most famous and popular book of the day, and it continued to find enthusiastic readers and reviewers and to sell astonishingly well for more than half a century.

## II   *A Christian Training*

The heroine of *The Wide, Wide World* is Ellen Montgomery, a young girl who has grown up in New York City in relatively fashionable and comfortable circumstances. Her father, at the beginning of the novel, has recently lost an important lawsuit and with it much of his fortune. In addition, his wife is in poor health, and in the hope of finding new sources of income and a place where her health will improve, he has decided to take her and travel abroad. Since his funds are limited, he has decided to leave his daughter in America and has arranged for her to live with his sister, Miss Fortune Emerson, in Thirlwall, a rural village far from the city. The opening chapters concern Ellen's separation from her mother and the subsequent journey to Thirlwall. Aunt Fortune or, as she is also called, Miss Fortune (the pun here is intentional) has little love for Ellen and considers her largely a nuisance until Ellen, during one of her aunt's illnesses, shows herself efficient and competent in running her aunt's domestic affairs. Meanwhile, Ellen is befriended by a neighboring farmer, Bram Van Brunt, who manages Aunt Fortune's farm and who later marries her. Among Ellen's other friends are Alice Humphreys and her brother John, a divinity student. They are the children of a local minister. Through the Humphreys, Ellen becomes friends with their relatives, the Marshman family, local gentry whose cultivated and cultured lives are compared by the author to the rustic lives and customs of Miss Fortune and her friends. A large portion of the book is spent contrasting a social "bee" at Miss Fortune's with the Marshman's elegant means of entertaining at Christmas.

Alice Humphreys dies, and Ellen, in obedience to one of Alice's last wishes, goes to live with Mr. Humphreys and his son in the hope of being daughter and sister to them. While abroad, Ellen's mother and father have died but have left a request that Ellen be sent to Scotland to live with her mother's family, the Lindsays. Ellen is sent to Scotland but hopes to return eventually to her friends in America and particularly to John. The concluding paragraph of the book suggests that eventually she will return to him and that they will be married.

The book is almost entirely lacking in dramatic incident or conflict. The narrative will inevitably seem discursive, rambling, to any reader unaware of the author's religious purpose or objective in writing the novel, for *The Wide, Wide World* is, first of all, a religious allegory, a sort of *Pilgrim's Progress* (a book that, notably, is among Ellen's favorites). The book traces Ellen's education as a Christian, and many of the central characters are models or emblems of such Christian virtues as patience, charity, and willing submission to divine purpose. Each character either contributes directly to Ellen's Christian education or tests that education by exposing Ellen to worldly values. Aunt Fortune and the Lindsays are as important to Ellen's education—and the narrative—as are Alice and John Humphreys, for it is in her conflicts with the former that she is able to prove herself as obedient and forgiving as the Humphreys have taught her to be. *The Wide, Wide World* is essentially a didactic novel; its purpose is to teach religious and moral values.

Susan's moral and religious values were those of nineteenth-century evangelical Christianity: charity, forbearance, sobriety, and submission to divine will and biblical authority, among others. In turn, these values dictated much of the novel's plot and characterization—a situation very different from that in the fiction of such contemporaries as, say, Nathaniel Hawthorne. In Hawthorne's works, a moral stance is used to *interpret* rather than *dictate* plot and characterization. This point is worth emphasizing, for it is basically this which, aside from differences in strictly literary merit, distinguishes *The Wide, Wide World* from books like *The Scarlet Letter.* In subject matter, both are, after all, religious novels, but Warner's is didactically so. Hawthorne interpreted his narrative from a moral perspective, but Warner began by devising a narrative that schematically illustrated her moral and religious beliefs. Even in her later books, which were all solidly based on historical incidents, narrative and characterization were shaped to didactic ends.

*The Wide, Wide World* traces its heroine's progress from a concern solely with worldly love—suggested by her devotion to her mother—to a concern with higher or spiritual love—suggested by, among other things, her devotion to the minister John Humphreys. Perhaps no passage in the book is liable to seem more extraordinary or incredible to modern readers than that in which one of the Marshmans tells the heroine that God has taken her mother from her because Ellen, in loving her mother so intensely, "was in danger of forgetting him, and he loved you, Ellen; . . . and now he says to you, 'My daughter, give *me* thy heart.' "[5] *The Wide, Wide World* contends that the true Christian will absolutely, unquestioningly, and unhesitatingly submit himself to divine will, especially divine will as revealed in the Bible. Above all, the Christian will allow no human affection to interfere with his devotion to his God.

### III  *The Domestic Dilemma*

The nineteenth century, as recent historical studies have shown, was preeminently an era of domesticity and close family life. Philip Aries and his followers have documented some of the effects that family life had on individual lives and civilization in general.[6] While historians may not agree on the reasons why family life became as important as it did, all agree that for the nineteenth century, domestic life was of overwhelming importance—a fact reflected in the literature of the time and a major concern of *The Wide, Wide World.* Susan Warner personally left no doubt that she, like her contemporaries, considered family life not only important to social life but central to an individual's spiritual and moral existence, and although she herself never married, her most famous novel is a didactic tale that preaches the values of family life.

Ellen's mother has no affection for her husband (nor does he have any for her), but neither she nor, for that matter, the author questions his absolute authority over his wife. Paul in his epistle to the Ephesians demanded, as Susan, of course, well knew, that wives "submit [themselves] unto [their] own husbands, as unto the Lord" and that children be similarly obedient to their parents.[7] Biblically, neither wife nor child is given the right to question the authority of the husband or father. Ellen has no love for her father and, after his death, remembers her experiences with him as "the least agreeable" part of her life.[8] Her father has neither her love nor his wife's affection, but he has their absolute obedience.

As part of her education, Ellen is told that she must learn to submit her will to her elders as unhesitatingly as her mother has submitted her will to her husband. Ellen must learn never to contradict her elders—or, eventually, her husband—even when she believes they are wrong. The novel suggests, however, that while Ellen may not contradict the will of an elder, she might conceivably disobey him if she believed that his will did not accord with some higher, divine purpose. For example, in the closing chapters of the novel, Ellen is sent to Scotland to live with her uncle and his family. The uncle insists that Ellen give him the respect and obedience that would be due a father, and Ellen agrees—with a condition. She is willing to be docile, obedient, and submissive to her uncle unless his will conflicts with what she knows, particularly as the result of studying her Bible, to be a higher purpose. She is willing to submit herself unconditionally only to men like John Humphreys, who wants to escape from the world and "the signs of man's presence and influence," and who is seldom content except when contemplating spiritual matters.[9]

Although *The Wide, Wide World* continually reasserts the importance of family life and particularly the absolute authority of the husband and father, the book also insists that this authority is his only when it does not conflict with what his wife and children consider divine will. In effect, he has no more free will or free choice than they, and his authority is valid only when it reflects God's purpose.

## IV   *Christian Nurture*

As we have seen, Susan's theological training was largely in evangelicalism, which insisted on an individual's attention to biblical authority and absolute submission to divine will. Her religious perspective was that of her minister, Thomas Harvey Skinner; and there is no record that she ever dissented from his opinions. She followed him even in defending religious ecumenicity—a relatively unpopular but open and liberal movement of the day. Certainly this movement deeply influenced her religious attitudes.

There were other sources for her theological premises. Among the theologians whom she read was Horace Bushnell, a liberal Congregationalist minister whose *Christian Nurture* (1846) argued that religious conversion could result not from a sudden awareness or awakening to divine grace—a theological point argued by Charles Grandison Finney and other influential revivalist ministers—but from a life-long training in Christian principles and attitudes. In turn, *The Wide, Wide World*, which was written and published during the years *Christian Nurture* was being widely condemned by conservative theologians, portrays the sort of religious training that Bushnell described. Ellen becomes a Christian not through a sudden awareness of divine grace but through an extensive education in Christian behavior—an education begun by her mother and carried out by members of the Marshman and Humphreys families. In terms of Protestant theological thinking at the time the novel was published, *The Wide, Wide World* must have seemed liberal indeed. *Christian Nurture*, after all, so upset the conservative clergy that Bushnell was very nearly tried for heresy.

## V   *Religion and Sales*

With good reason, readers today may wonder why a novel so intensely moralistic and pietistic should also have been one of the most extraordinarily popular books ever published. Of course, religious novels can still be found on best-seller lists, but these novels are generally more concerned with religious, usually biblical, history than with theological matters such as those that dictated so much of the narrative and characterization in *The Wide, Wide World*.

The best sellers of the nineteenth century, particularly the latter half of the century, are often marked by biblical and theological concerns no less abstruse than those that concerned Susan Warner. *The Gates Ajar* by Elizabeth Stuart Phelps sketched out with much theological pedantry a materialistic heaven to which any middle-class American could aspire, and E. P. Roe's *Barriers Burned Away* (1872) used an exceedingly melodramatic plot involving the Chicago Fire to make more palatable (or exciting) what was essentially a sermon on Christian values. Charles M. Sheldon's *In His Steps* (1896) taught its readers to make in their lives the sort of decisions that Christ would have made. Novels based on biblical history also enjoyed huge audiences. Lew Wallace's *Ben Hur* (1880) sold two-and-a-half million copies. Earlier best-selling biblical novels included Joseph Holt Ingraham's *The Prince of the House of David* (1855). In addition, domestic novelists, like Susan Warner, were often religious novelists as well, and their worship of domesticity was tied to a belief in the religious values that domestic life was supposed to entail. Maria Cummins's *The Lamplighter* (1854) and Augusta Jane Evans's *St. Elmo* (1867) are very nearly as drenched in religiosity as *The Wide, Wide World*. Most of what we consider best in nineteenth-century American literature is also largely concerned with moral or religious problems. *Moby—Dick* and *The Scarlet Letter*, to cite two of the more prominent examples, are as concerned with morals and metaphysics as any of the more popular novels of the time.

## VI  *A Sense of Time and Place*

*The Wide, Wide World*'s religious orientation was responsible for much, perhaps most, of the critical attention that it received, but critics, especially those who wrote for literary journals like *The North American Review* and *The Literary World*, also had considerable praise for its detailed descriptions of rural life. This second factor, the novel's local color, still attracts literary attention today. *The Wide, Wide World* depends heavily for its sense of time and place on the author's knowledge of Yankee and upstate New York customs and dialect. As a record of New England life, the novel was in fact matched by no contemporaries and few successors. The book's didactic lessons are dramatized through highly realistic details of characterization. Ellen, Alice, John, and some of the other characters may seem too ideal, too pure to satisfy readers, but these improbably perfect figures are balanced by others—particularly Aunt Fortune, Mr. Van Brunt, and the townspeople in Thirlwall—who are graphically and realistically characterized. Intended primarily as emblems of spiritual and moral values, figures like Alice and John have no psychological vitality—or validity—but Aunt Fortune and others like her are realistically portrayed in terms of regional dialect and manners.

*The Wide, Wide World* continues to receive critical attention largely because it is one of the earliest and best examples of local-color writing, but unlike most local color fiction, it is unsympathetic to the rural life and manners it portrays. In general, local colorists approached regional customs with nostalgia. Sarah Orne Jewett, for example, lovingly described rural values and customs which had been usurped by urban values and customs which she found distasteful. But Susan Warner, like Edith Wharton a half-century later, considered rural New England to be morally barren—a region of practical, utilitarian thought where human affection had no place.

Susan Warner's knowledge of New England (and her dislike of it) resulted from childhood experiences. When she was a young girl, she was sent, against her will, to spend her summers at the old Warner homestead not far from the Massachusetts border in upstate New York. But, for a young lady of fashion, this was unwelcome exile. Her experiences in the country deserve special attention, since they not only provided her with much valuable material for her fiction but also determined that aversion to Yankee life that is found in most of her local-color writings.

## VII  *A New Canaan*

The large, rambling farmhouse where the Warner children spent several summers had been built by their grandfather, Jason Warner, and was located in Canaan, New York. The Warners had been among the town's earliest settlers and had prospered there as farmers. Jason left the town briefly to serve with his father in the Revolutionary War and later represented his region in the state legislature, but most of his life was spent in Canaan. It was the only town in which Susan Warner's father lived before he left for college and his subsequent legal career in New York. The Warners were closely identified with Canaan, but it was an identification which

Susan, as a fashionable young lady, at times wished to hide or forget. Much more to her taste were the mansion and elegant estate of her grandfather Bogert.

The Warners were descended from Pilgrim and Puritan colonists, and although the Canaan homestead was technically located in New York State, the few miles that separated the house from the Massachusetts border did not prevent the family from thinking of themselves as Yankees or New Englanders. When they moved to Canaan in 1764, they brought with them their New England Calvinism. Members of first the Congregational and later the Presbyterian church, the Warners had little reason, in either religion or ancestry, to consider themselves New Yorkers. They had little contact either with Dutch New Yorkers or with the Dutch Reformed and Anglican churches that prevailed in most of New York. As late as 1909, when Anna Warner was in her eighties and had never lived more than a few months within New England's geographic boundaries, she described herself as a New Englander.[10]

Canaan itself was essentially a New England village. To the east, the town bordered on Massachusetts, and only by geographical accident were the Canaanites Yorkers rather than Yankees. When Susan wrote about Canaan, as she did in both *The Wide, Wide World* and *Queechy*, she wrote in effect about a New England town, and it is as a New England local colorist that she should be studied. The first of the New England local colorists—and Susan Warner's only major predecessor—was Catharine Maria Sedgwick, who wrote about Stockbridge and other Massachusetts villages twenty miles to the east of Canaan. Stockbridge and Canaan were similar in so many respects—heritage, customs, dialect—that the two authors found themselves utilizing virtually the same materials in their fiction. But there was this major difference: while Miss Sedgwick, at least in her later works, wrote with affection and nostalgia about New Englanders, Susan Warner generally treated them with disapproval or condescension.

The worlds she preferred were to be found in books and New York drawing-rooms. The heroines of *The Wide, Wide World* and *Queechy* spend much time walking in the meadows and woods, but when visiting her grandfather, Susan Warner had always preferred to stay inside with her books. "Her nervous imagination," Anna recalled, "fostered this indoor life; with slippery hills, and creeping things, and strange wayfarers along the road,—all sorts of unknown possibilities everywhere,—the sheltering walls of the house seemed delightful, and she left them as little as she could."[11] After spending the summer at her grandfather's when she was seventeen, she wrote, "I do not love Canaan very much most certainly, and shouldn't care much if I thought we should not spend another summer here."[12] A visit to the Shaker community in the neighboring town of Lebanon had been proposed, but it held no interest for her: "How much better worth it is to stay quietly at home and read Cowper, than to see all the Shakers in the world."[13] (And this from an author who was to describe the Shakers at length many years later in *Queechy*.)

After her grandfather's death in 1841, the sisters no longer visited Canaan, and over the years, her attitude toward rural New England softened, although her condescension toward New Englanders never completely vanished. Ten years after *The Wide, Wide World* was published, she visited a friend in Lenox, a small Massachusetts village a few miles east of Canaan. "What air! what lakes and hills! what Canaan reminiscences!" she wrote. "It is lovely out of doors and in; . . . It is all so good to us!"[14] One would not guess that the same writer had once "cared not very much for the natural world" but had instead been "eagerly fond of society."[15] Susan Warner never escaped entirely her prejudice against Yankees and New England, but the Yankees in her last novels—notably the heroine of *My Desire*—are treated at times with a respect that no one who has read *The Wide, Wide World* might expect.

## VIII  *Reality and Fiction*

Contrary to what some of its first reviewers assumed, *The Wide, Wide World* is not autobiographical. She did, however, draw heavily on her memories of life in Canaan and on her grandfather's farm. The Emerson farmhouse is, for example, based on her grandfather's. She turned the house on its axis to face east rather than west and extended the distance from house to town by a few miles, but in other respects she described her grandfather's house and its setting with photographic fidelity. Likewise, she faithfully recorded Canaan customs and dialect, particularly in Chapters twenty-four and twenty-five. These chapters concern Aunt Fortune's "bee," at which the townspeople, in return for food and drink, help her with various farm chores. The following passage is representative of the dialogue in this episode. The setting is Aunt Fortune's house, and the speakers are her guests.

"Girls! girls!—what *are* you leaving the door open for!"—sounded from the kitchen, and they [Ellen and a neighbor, Nancy Vawse] hurried in.

" 'most got through [paring apples], Nancy?" inquired Bob Lawson. . . .

"Ha'n't begun to, Mr. Lawson. There's every bit as many to do as there was at your house t'other night."

"What on airth does she want with such a sight of 'em," inquired Dan Dennison.

"Live on pies and apple-sass till next summer," suggested Mimy Lawson.

"That's the stuff for my money!" replied her brother; " 'taters and apple-sass is my sass in the winter."

"It's good those is easy got," said his sister Mary; "the sass is the most of the dinner to Bob most commonly."

"Are they fixing for more apple-sass down stairs?" Mr. Dennison went on rather dryly.

"No—hush!"—said Juniper Hitchcock,—"sassages!"

"Humph!" said Dan, as he speared up an apple out of the basket on the point of his knife,—"ain't that something like what you call killing two—" [He means here that people at a "bee" should be assigned one task, not two as is the case here.]

"Just that exactly," said Jenny Hitchcock, as Dan broke off sho.    ınd the mistress of the house walked in. "Ellen," she whispered, "don't you want to go down stairs and see when the folks are coming up to help us? And tₑll the doctor he must be spry, for we ain't a go'ng to get through in a hurry," she added, laughing.[16]

When Susan was writing about the people of Thirlwall, her own diction became at times more natural and colloquial than in the rest of the novel. Among the colloquial expressions that she introduced are "no sooner said than done," "neat as a pin," "neat as wax," and "apple-pie order."[17] A hearth is "clean swept up"; a room full of people is "in a complete hurly-burly"; and another room is "as neat as hands [can] make it."[18] Ellen is "fevered with [a] notion"; Alice is "chatting away"; and Ellen's grandmother talks "as much as she [has] a mind."[19] Mr. Van Brunt is "no mean hand; his slices of ham [are] very artist-like, and frying away in the most unexceptionable manner."[20] One person is said to be "all eyes," while another's face is "a real refreshment," and another's is "very dead-and-alive."[21] Ellen is "kept on the jump a great deal of the time"; eggs are "scrambled to a nicety"; and a particular incident is "enough to set the whole neighbourhood a wondering."[22]

There is nothing consistent about the colloquial diction; it may be found on one page and not on the next. With few exceptions, however, the colloquialisms are limited to passages dealing with Aunt Fortune and the townspeople, and there is good reason to believe that the author's shift to colloquial diction in these passages was entirely unplanned and unconscious. Certainly her contemporaries did not approve of the colloquialisms, which one reviewer called "certain specimens of homeliness in diction," "sad blemishes" on the book.[23] In fact, the book makes plain the fact that the author herself considered colloquial language disagreeable. Alice, for example, is distressed whenever Ellen uses poor English or colloquial language, and John corrects Ellen when she says she has "fixed [herself] . . . nicely on the sofa," when she should have said "arranged" or "established."[24] John and Alice would surely have been distressed to find their author saying of Mr. Van Brunt that "he was beating his brains the whole way to think of something it would do to say."[25] No less distressing would have been the "sentence," "Then fell a fumbling in his pocket."[26] The statement is understandable and effective in the passage in which it occurs, but Alice and John (and, had she thought about it, the author herself) would have been distressed by the fact that it is both colloquial and grammatically incorrect. As contemporary reviews of *The Wide, Wide World* suggest, the colloquial language that readers now consider colorful were then thought to be in very poor taste.

Alice always speaks what the author felt was perfect English. Much is made of Alice's having grown up in England where her language was not tainted by Yankee expressions, yet today that language seems stilted and impersonal. In one episode, Alice, concerned that her father may be wondering where she is, tells Mr. Van Brunt, "I shall be greatly obliged if you will be so kind as to stop and relieve my father's anxiety."[27] It is refreshing, by contrast, to hear Aunt Fortune tell her niece, "Well, ask [your question] then quick, and have done, and take yourself off. I have other fish to fry than to answer all your questions."[28]

## IX   *Yankee vs. Yorker*

Aunt Fortune and Mr. Van Brunt conform, respectively, to two folk types common to nineteenth-century American literature: the Yankee and the Yorker. James Fenimore Cooper's *Satanstoe* (1845), for example, has much to say about Yankees and Yorkers (at the Yankees' expense), and in Washington Irving's "The Legend of Sleepy Hollow" (1820), the schoolmaster Ichabod Crane is Yankee,

and his rival, Brom Bones, is a Yorker. Yankees in American fiction
are descendants of the early New England settlers, from whom
(although this is not the case with Aunt Fortune) they often inherit
a highly religious and superstitious nature. They are also shrewd,
crafty, and practical, and they are usually good businessmen. Like
other Yankees in fiction, Aunt Fortune is remarkably efficient and
businesslike. Her farm is well run. She allows herself no frills and is
practical and shrewd in all her undertakings. Her dislike for her
niece is tempered only by Ellen's willingness to help with the
housework, and she marries Mr. Van Brunt because it is more efficient to run their respective farms as a single operation.

By contrast, Mr. Van Brunt, like other Yorkers in American fiction, is warm and sympathetic. He has inherited the generosity,
honesty, and affectionate nature of his ancestors, the original Dutch
settlers of New York. He shares Aunt Fortune's practicality and
good business sense—indeed he is the better businessman—but
never allows financial or practical matters to interfere with his
friendship with Ellen or other people in Thirlwall. Nonetheless, his
country manners place him in a category far below Alice, John, and
Ellen, and the novel treats him with much condescension. In one
episode, in which he takes Ellen by ox-cart from the center of the
town to Aunt Fortune's farm, he is called "he of the ox-cart" and
the "rough charioteer."[29] Ellen, accustomed to genteel city life, is
distressed to find Mr. Van Brunt, a common farmer, eating with her
at the same table—a distress that the fastidious author undoubtedly
thought justified.[30] Characterization eventually triumphs over
didacticism, however; Mr. Van Brunt's practicality and rugged
honesty may seem today far more attractive than Ellen's smug
idealism or Alice's perfect manners and stylized diction.

## X    The Right People

Alice and John Humphreys and their father provide Ellen with
examples of moral and spiritual ideals, while Mr. Van Brunt offers
practical examples of honesty and kindness. In addition, the
Marshman family is used to illustrate hospitality, social grace,
courtesy, and other social values. The Marshmans, who may have
been based on Susan's mother's family, are the author's ideal
aristocrats—people of exquisite manners and fine moral sensibilities.

The Marshman estate, Ventnor, is apparently situated (the exact geography is vague) near the Hudson in Dutchess or Columbia County—a region which for more than a century had been widely known for its vast country estates, most of which were owned by the Livingston family, with whom the Warners were good friends. (The Livingston estates also provided the settings for *Wych Hazel* and *The Gold of Chickaree*, which Susan and Anna later wrote together.[31]) However, the Christmas celebration that Ellen attends at Ventnor may well have been drawn after similar celebrations at the Bogert family estate in Jamaica, Long Island.

Mr. and Mrs. Marshman are "of stately presence, and most dignified as well as kind in their deportment"—a description that accords well, incidentally, with what we know of Cornelius Bogert and his wife.[32] One of the Marshman daughters, Mrs. Chauncy, is "a lady with a sweet, gentle, quiet face and manner," while another, Mrs. Gillespie, has "her mother's stately bearing," and the third, Sophia Marshman, is "lively and agreeable and good-humoured."[33] One imagines that in various Bogerts can be found these aristocratic women, that, for example, Susan's mother may have been the model for Mrs. Chauncy, and that Mrs. Chauncy's daughter, Ellen, is the author's idealized portrait of herself as a young lady.

The Marshmans' generosity and hospitality are extended to all who share their good breeding and manners. They treat Ellen as an equal, and neither do they display pride in their wealth and ancestry, nor do they ever use these things as yardsticks to measure social class. Above all, they share their good fortune with others—or at least with those whose conduct defines them as ladies or gentlemen. Their world of perfect manners is the social equivalent of the Humphreys' ideal moral and spiritual realm.

## XI  *The Critics*

*The Wide, Wide World*'s moral and religious ideals were immediately and widely praised by critics. The *Literary World* concluded that the novel's "religious teachings are worthy of all praise from their gentleness and earnestness, and the happy manner in which they are introduced."[34] John S. Hart compared aspects of the novel with the works of Daniel Defoe, then went on to say that this book was "the only novel in which real religious truth, at least as understood by evangelical Christians, is exhibited with truth."[35] Even reviewers who were generally unfavorable to the book spoke well of its religious intentions. In *Holden's Dollar Magazine*, the reviewer took issue with Alice and John's lengthy homilies and Ellen's "incessant blubbering"—in fact, she spends much of her time in tears. He hoped that the author's next book would "contain less dry logic and more dry land," yet he also insisted that the book was "wholly and unmistakably good . . . moral and religious instruction."[36] There were few who agreed, at least in print, with the reviewer who thought that this novel and *Queechy* were offensive in their "too frequent and even violent introduction of peculiar religious sentiments."[37]

Among the novel's admirers was Henry James, who described it favorably in an 1865 issue of *The Nation*. He was especially interested in the novel's realistic evocation of rural life, and he thought that as a transcription of local color, it was more successful than the novels of Flaubert. There are surely few who would defend James's conclusion today, but it does suggest the enormous critical esteem that *The Wide, Wide World* once enjoyed.[38]

Frank Denham, discussing the novel several years ago in the *New York Times Book Review*, said that "Miss Warner thought herself a realist, but her characters were not real people because she never let herself know what people were really like."[39] The statement is a curious one, unsupported by a close reading of the novel. James was accurate in noting the book's excellent sense of local color and realistic detail. Among recent critics, Henry Nash Smith finds, "amid the interminable tears and prayers," "well-executed genre scenes";[40] another has said that "it is essential to read some of [Warner's books] in order to have a complete picture of American social life in the nineteenth century."[41]

Although nineteenth-century critics almost universally agreed that the novel was a masterpiece, twentieth-century critics have violently attacked it, particularly for its piety and sentimentality. Van Wyck Brooks dismissed it as "malarial," "a swamp of lachrymosity,"[42] While Frank Luther Mott said it fit a "Home-and-Jesus formula" and was, "at best, mawkish in its sentimentality and pious to a repulsive degree."[43] Such exteme reactions tell us more about the prejudices of the critics involved than about the book itself; they are also the exceptions. Neither Matthew Arnold nor Charles Kingsley, it is true, thought highly of the book (Kingsley called it *The Narrow, Narrow World* and retitled its successors *Squeeky* and *The Hills of the Chattermuch*),[44] but there have been other critics who have strongly or warmly defended it. George Saintsbury recalled the book "with pleasure,"[45] and the American critic Brander Matthews listed it, together with works by Sir Walter Scott, Charles Dickens, and George Eliot, as one of the "hundred Best Novels in English."[46]

## XII   *The Readers*

In a recent article on the Warners, Grace Overmyer claims that *The Wide, Wide World* was "the first American best seller,"[47] and even though the records of book selling in the nineteenth century are notoriously incomplete and unreliable, the novel's success in this country was apparently unprecedented. Overmyer's claim is not entirely accurate—there were, of course, many American novels before 1850 that were best sellers, but certainly no American book had ever sold so well.

The book was also very popular abroad. More than two dozen English publishers issued separate editions. Since publishers' records in Britain, like those in America, have been lost or destroyed, the total sales will never be known; but we know that one publisher, Routledge, sold eighty thousand copies, an astonishing figure for the time. The book remained popular with all classes; and forty years after it first appeared, it was, with the Bible, "one of the four books most widely read in England."[48] One investigator who set out to discover "what . . . English peasants read" concluded that *The Wide, Wide World* was, together with *Pilgrim's Progress* and *Uncle Tom's Cabin*, among their favorite books.[49] According to a poll taken in 1886, English schoolgirls rated Susan Warner's novels above those by George Eliot, Harriet Beecher Stowe, William Makepeace Thackeray, and Charlotte Brontë. "*The Wide, Wide World* and *Queechy*," one critic wrote, "give place to no books in the English language for popularity among girls old and young."[50] The book was translated several times, and editions appeared bearing the titles, *Heimwärts: oder Führung durch die Weite Welt*, *Den Vide, Vide Verden*, and *Le monde, le vaste monde*. In 1876, a contributor to *The Nation* commented that Frenchmen and Germans who claimed to know something about American literature often turned out to have read only *The Wide, Wide World*.[51]

## XIII  *Why It Sold*

Neither its author nor its publisher anticipated the novel's
success, and its popularity is still difficult to explain. If nineteenth-
century reviews and comments are a reliable index to popular opinion, *The Wide, Wide World* was admired and read because of its
evangelical bias, its attitude toward family life, and its record of
rural American life and customs. The novel's didacticism was far
more important to its popular reception than was its literary value,
and the thematic ingredients that insured its popular success were
soon recognized by other writers. Evangelical Christian doctrine,
local color, and domesticity are central to many later best sellers, including novels by Maria Cummins, Augusta Jane Evans, and E.P.
Roe which, like *The Wide, Wide World*, sold in the hundreds of
thousands.

Hiram Haydn, one of the most respected editors of our time, once
read several of Lloyd C. Douglas's religious novels in order to discover why they "sold by the carloads."[52] He discovered a
"passionate conviction . . . manifest on every page" that not only
"persuaded the reader" but also sold the books.[53] A similar
"passionate conviction" is characteristic of Susan Warner's novels
and, for that matter, the novels of most best-selling, nineteenth-
century religious writers. Without that conviction, didactic religious
fiction is often dry, obviously schematic, and unconvincing. Didactic fiction does not transcribe human nature realistically but
arranges characterization to illustrate principles or ideas. If,
however, a "passionate conviction" underscores those principles or
ideas, the novel may convey an intensity that compensates for weak
plotting and improbable characterization.

*The Wide, Wide World* should not be criticized according to
twentieth-century standards: both its purpose and its reception can
be understood only within its historical setting, but presentist
critics—critics, that is, who interpret past literatures in terms of
present-day standards and interests—have, from time to time,
offered ingenious explanations for the book's popular success; on
close examination, these explanations, however, prove themselves
textually and historically questionable. One critic—whose sense of
nineteenth-century cultural history is generally excellent—falls into
the presentist trap by declaring that *The Wide, Wide World* was
popular because, among other things, it "provided its ready

audience with every one of the five Jungian archetypes"[54]—an explanation that may satisfy few except Jungian critics. The book has also been misread as a popular appeal to a nascent feminist sensibility, and because the book is central to an understanding of women's literary and cultural history, this interpretation deserves particular notice.

### XIV   Women's Rights

Helen Waite Papashvily suggested in her study of domestic novels, *All the Happy Endings* (1956), that *The Wide, Wide World* responded to the sensibilities of women who believed themselves dominated, against their wills, by husbands, brothers, fathers, or other men. Papashvily's book is widely respected and has influenced subsequent studies of domestic novels. *All the Happy Endings* is an exceptionally important study of nineteenth-century American culture, but Papashvily is mistaken in including *The Wide, Wide World* among feminist novels. Susan Warner's attitude toward the social and domestic position of women was, as we have seen, quite different from what Papashvily suggests.

*All the Happy Endings* argues that while mid-nineteenth-century feminists were rallying around the Seneca Falls "Declaration of Sentiments" (that extraordinary document that claimed that throughout history men had tried to establish "an absolute tyranny" over women), their more conservative sisters were reading domestic novels which, however innocuous they seemed on the surface, were "a witches' broth, a lethal draught brewed by women and used by women to destroy their common enemy, man."[55] Papashvily suggests that *The Wide, Wide World* was part of that "lethal draught" and that the novel is at least in part about an unjustifiable submission of women to men. Nothing could be further from the truth.

Some of the domestic novels, particularly Mrs. E.D.E.N. Southworth's, seem to fit Papashvily's formula; but throughout Susan's works, she insisted that traditional husband and wife relationships were virtuous and just, because biblically sanctioned. Papashvily is correct in assuming that the readers of *The Wide, Wide World* were largely women; but if these women, as she assumes, read the book because of its message, they sought a lesson in obedience, submission, and sobriety. In fact, since evangelical

Christianity, which made of obedience a virtue, pervaded the
nineteenth century, it is likely that the lesson that the novel taught
was a lesson its readers had already learned well.

The Wide, Wide World is of major significance to an understanding of America at mid-century. It is tempting, but ultimately misleading, to interpret the era in the conflicting terms of Emersonian
optimism and Melvillian skepticism. The extraordinary, sympathetic reception that The Wide, Wide World received implies a
substantial audience which shared neither extreme—an audience
which, above all, valued sobriety, temperance, and obedience to
divine will. And the book's great popularity also suggests that the
Seneca Falls "Declaration of Sentiments" was historically a far
more eccentric document than some historians, in retrospect, would
make it seem.

## XV    The Domestic Novel

The Wide, Wide World is one of the first, and certainly the most
famous, domestic novel—a type of didactic novel that preached the
virtues of family life and that became a staple of best-seller lists in
the second half of the nineteenth century. Read principally by
women, these novels were directed at a Protestant audience which
considered the family ideally a moral bastion. Evangelical morality
and piety were usually preached, although occasionally a writer like
Mrs. Southworth was too busy with her sensational or melodramatic
plots to worry about moral or metaphysical implications. Most
domestic novels, including The Wide, Wide World showed the influence of eighteenth-century sentimental fiction, Hannah More's
didactic tales, and the evangelical, Low-Church novels popular in
England. Low-Church novels, it is true, were frequently more sensational and sentimental than their American kin, and they were
also more explicitly didactic, but they shared an evangelical bias
and invariably interpreted experience morally.

The earliest American domestic novelist was Catharine Maria
Sedgwick. In the 1820s and 1830s, she combined domestic life with
local color to create novels whose success was as unexpected as the
success of The Wide, Wide World. Miss Sedgwick wrote, however,
from a Unitarian perspective which stressed freedom of the individual conscience rather than obedience to authority. The moral
position was unacceptable both to Calvinism and evangelicalism;
and the novels, although widely praised and admired for their pic-

tures of American life, never had sales as spectacular as those of *The Wide, Wide World*.

Susan Warner's novel is in some respects similar to Miss Sedgwick's *A New-England Tale* (1822). Indeed, in broad terms, the plots are almost identical—and both novels make considerable use of New England local color. In both books, an unquestionably moral young girl is left an orphan shortly after her father loses his fortune. Both girls are then cared for by aunts who are blind to their nieces' moral natures and unfairly accuse them of wrongdoing. In the end, however, both heroines are married to men as virtuous as they and are promised an ideal family life. Susan Warner, of course, develops her plot to illustrate moral principles that her predecessor would have found unacceptable; yet there are so many similarities between the two novels that *A New-England Tale* seems almost certainly to have been a model for *The Wide, Wide World*.

Miss Sedgwick's novel, it is true, was published a quarter of a century before Susan Warner began work on hers, but she may have remembered the book from childhood; for in its day, *A New-England Tale* would have seemed, along with the works of Maria Edgeworth and Hannah More, appropriate didactic fare for children.

Although *A New-England Tale* may have been a model for *The Wide, Wide World* Susan did not, however, read Miss Sedgwick's other domestic novels, *Redwood* (1824) and *Clarence* (1835) until *The Wide, Wide World* was finished and being set in type. She read the novels at her publisher's suggestion. Putnam was then issuing a uniform edition of Miss Sedgwick's writings; and in his wife's phrase, he considered her to be "a piece of perfection."[56] Mrs. Putnam did not agree—nor, after reading these novels, did Susan. "Miss Sedgwick's novels are *inexpressible*," she told her sister; these two books in particular were "dismally poor."[57]

The many parallels, both in subject matter and literary treatment, between Miss Sedgwick's novels and *The Wide, Wide World* make this harsh criticism appear startling and unexpected. Certainly Miss Sedgwick had cleared the literary ground that Susan occupied, but theologically they stood opposed to each other, and from Susan's moral stance and religious position, Miss Sedgwick's novels could only seem morally weak or misleading. In the end, a book's value, for people like Susan, was to be judged solely on religious and moral, not literary, grounds.[58]

CHAPTER 3

# Learning To Be a Lady

W E have no privileged class—we have no American aristocracy! Heaven forbid we ever should, other than that truly
republican one, the aristocracy of mind and manners.
—Susan Warner, "How May an American Woman Best Show Her
Patriotism" (1850)[1]

In this privileged land, where we acknowledge no distinctions but what are
founded on character and manners, she is a lady, who, to in-bred modesty
and refinement, adds a scrupulous attention to the rights and feelings of
others. Let her worldly possessions be great or small, let her occupations be
what they may, such an one is a lady, a gentlewoman. Whilst the person
who is bold, coarse, vociferous, and inattentive to the rights and feelings of
others, is a vulgar woman, let her possessions be ever so great, and her way
of living ever so genteel. Thus we may see a lady sewing for her livelihood,
and a vulgar woman presiding over a most expensive establishment.
—Mrs. John Farrar, *The Young Lady's Friend* (1838)[2]

## I  *Ghosts*

George Haven Putnam was six years old when Susan Warner, at
his father's invitation, descended on the Putnam household on
Staten Island to spend a few weeks while correcting the proofs of
*The Wide, Wide World.* Since Haven, as he was called by his
parents, was the oldest boy, he was allowed to have dinner with
their guest and the other adults, but neither he nor his brothers and
sisters were welcome at breakfast or tea. "I like that very well I
must say," Susan remarked to her sister. "What possibility of conversation is there at a table where four or five children are to be
attended to?"[3]

For his part, Haven remembered this rather towering
woman—"nearly six feet in height"—in equally unflattering terms.
"I have a picture of a long head surmounting a long neck," he said

54

more than sixty years later, "and of a bowing or swaying motion which at times gave the impression of an affectation of graciousness"—affected graciousness, not the real thing.[4] "Excepting for an occasional and very brief visit to New York," this literary guest from up the Hudson "could hardly, at the time she began the writing of her books, have seen anything whatsoever of the world of society."[5]

Susan Warner must herself have been acutely aware of how provincial she seemed not only to Haven but also to other members of the family and their friends. A decade earlier the Warners had fled the city in economic disgrace. When money permitted, they returned to New York for the winter months, but there were few friends there to welcome them. As a child, Susan had not wanted to leave the city for a summer visit to the country, but now it was the city that she wished to avoid. She told her sister of one train trip entering New York "past the many, many stacks of boards and lumber piled along the wharves, poor-looking men, and poor-looking boys, and sad-looking dwelling places—Oh the city,—and the suburbs of the city—they are not pleasant, Annie. I felt as I walked slowly up Broadway that I had left the best part of the world behind me."[6]

The visit to the Putnams was not entirely something to look forward to. They occupied an elegant villa overlooking New York bay, managed a staff of servants, and in general lived the sort of genteel life that the Warners had once known but which had long since been replaced by the comparatively barren and uneventful life of Constitution Island. Anna, in her biography of her sister, could not remember what was packed for clothes on the visit but thought that "the furnishing must have been but scanty."[7] There was a wide social gap between the Putnams and their guest, and friendly though her host and hostess were, that fact could not be disguised. In the end, Susan left the Putnams before her work on the proofs was completed. Some ladies were expected to come to dinner and spend the night, and the Putnams protested that it was not necessary for their guest to leave, but, as she wrote to Anna, "I knew it was best."[8]

During her stay at the Putnams, perhaps nothing so painfully underscored the change in her social position than a visit to the home of Mrs. David Codwise, one of the few friends from the past who still corresponded with the Warners. The Codwise villa was a short walk from the Putnam house, and soon after her arrival, Susan wrote excitedly to Anna that she might have an opportunity to meet their old friend. A week passed before an opportunity presented itself. The weather was "entirely exquisite," and so after breakfast, she tied on her bonnet and took the road to her friend's. But when she got there, she found no one at home, the house shut up, and the gates padlocked. No one had thought to tell her that her friend had moved back to the city. "There is a melancholy look about a place in such a condition," she wrote to Anna, "especially one where you have known happy times."[9]

A few weeks after returning from the Putnams to Constitution Island, Susan began work on her second novel, *Queechy*, in part a record of the fashionable New York she once had known. Conceivably, the book was begun in response to her visit to the Putnams; during her visit, she met friends she had long forgotten and experienced a type of life she had once known. But what that brief visit did not tell her was the great degree to which New York had changed since the Warners sold their mansion on St. Mark's Place. Hundreds of prominent New York families, like the Warners, had been ruined in the Panic of 1837, and by 1850, their social place had been taken by new families headed, in most cases, by merchants and professionals—with no allegiance or tie to the New York that the Warners had known. Of course, many—perhaps most—of the old families remained influential in social matters; yet the changes which had taken place were decided. A few weeks at the Putnams were not enough to tell her how great those changes were; and as a result, while *Queechy* was ostensibly set in the present (the 1840s and 1850s), it described a New York that had largely vanished a decade earlier. Critics were quick to note the apparent inaccuracy of her descriptions of fashionable life; but the criticism must have only bewildered the author, who, describing things as they had been, may have believed that she was describing things as they still were.

## II   *The Village of Fashion*

Before examining *Queechy*, it is important to study at close range the social and geographic perimeters of the aristocratic world it characterizes. The aristocracy that the Warners knew was the aristocracy of the 1830's; and two decades later, when the sisters were publishing their first books, society was already abandoning St. Mark's Place and the other fashionable addresses that the Warners had known—Great Jones Street, Bleecker Street, Lafayette

Place (now Lafayette Street), Bond Street, Stuyvesant Street, and other streets in that section of New York known today as Astor Place and the East Village. By the time Susan Warner died in 1885, St. Mark's Place and the streets around it were lined, in fact, with run-down boarding houses, warehouses, and factories. Here and there one found privately owned townhouses in which old families lived in reduced circumstances, too poor to follow their richer friends in the city's relentless march northward.

When the Warners lived at St. Mark's Place, nearby Bond Street was, according to Henry T. Tuckerman, "the 'up-town' centre of the most eligible private residences"; and only "down-town's" Hudson Square might compete for social precedence. Bond Street "was the scene of the choicest social enjoyment. Lined with trees, in the early summer, the lamps gleaming among the trees, [it] reminded one of Paris." [10] Here lived Dr. John Wakefield Francis, a man at the very center of the city's literary and social life and a friend of the Warners. Down the street in what was undoubtedly the city's largest and most elegant mansion lived another of the Warners' friends, Samuel Ward, senior partner in the great banking firm of Prime, Ward, King, and Company. His daughter Julia was among Susan Warner's closest childhood friends. The future author of "The Battle Hymn of the Republic" was then as much a lady of fashion as was Susan Warner and was known, together with her two sisters, as one of the "Three Graces of Bond Street."

Livingstons, Schermerhorns, Ruggleses, Gallatins, and Lorillards also lived on Bond Street, and nearby at Lafayette Place were Delanos and Astors. John Jacob Astor was probably the richest man in the country, and his presence behind the Corinthian columns of LaGrange Terrace must have been comforting to those residents who needed the assurance that they lived in the very best section of the city. If Astor gave the area the blessing of wealth, the Stuyvesants gave it the blessing of tradition and age. Their townhouses—like, incidentally, the Warners'—occupied land that had been part of the "bouwerie" or farm of Governor Peter Stuyvesant a century and a half earlier.

The Warner house was larger than most of the townhouses on the surrounding streets. Built of brick, it was three bays wide and five stories tall. Sandstone steps with cast-iron railings led to a doorway outlined with fine Federal detailing. Inside, one found expensive carpets, curtains, and furniture—all in crimson or crimson and drab—that exactly reflected, like the paintings which lined the walls, the best taste of the day. Behind the house were flower gardens and a greenhouse—rare luxuries in the crowded city—as well as a carriage house.

The Warner children spent most of their days in lessons and in social visits. Social life in the 1830's was quite tame compared to later decades. Conversation was especially valued, and so afternoon visits and evening gatherings were looked forward to as occasions on which to demonstrate wit or clever repartee—although, as James Fenimore Cooper showed in *Home As Found* (1838), these conversations were somewhat less clever than the participants thought. Young ladies were supposed to have some accomplishment to demonstrate at social gatherings, and Susan, who considered herself a poor conversationalist, was from time to time called on to play the piano. But she had an equally low estimate of herself as a pianist, and once when she was a guest at the Ward mansion, she hid the sheet music so that she couldn't be called on to play.

A fashionable young lady like Susan Warner would have spent part of most days riding about the city in one of the family carriages. A ride to Washington Square was especially pleasant. There were also private lessons—the Warners' Italian teacher was the Mozart librettist Lorenzo Da Ponte—and much time was given to reading. The Sabbath was, of course, strictly observed. When not in church, the Warners generally spent their time reading the Bible or other appropriate books.

A generation later, social entertaining in New York was far more lavish than anything Susan knew as a child. (In turn, entertaining in turn-of-the-century New York, as Edith Wharton was to note, greatly outdid anything in the 1850's.) Balls became more common—much to the horror of the puritanical families like the Warners—and formal dinners began to replace social teas and evening gatherings for conversation as the principal form of entertainment. The later generation also gave less attention to education and religion. The Sabbath was still observed, of course, but society chose its churches, of which Grace Church was the most famous, on the basis of the wealth, rather than the piety, of their congregations. Once in the 1830's, Susan Warner and her aunt ran up a bill of more than a hundred dollars—more than a thousand in today's currency—for dresses at A.T. Stewart's; but a generation later would have found the sum insufficient for a single outfit for an important occasion. The rich not only had more money but also far more extravagant ways of spending it.

The area around St. Mark's place deteriorated quickly after 1850; and according to one exposé of low life in the city, Bleecker Street, where "stately drawing rooms" had once "welcomed brilliant assemblages," was by 1870 "a suspicious neighborhood, to say the least, and he who frequents it must be prepared for the gossip and surmises of his friends."[11] "Mrs. Grundy now shivers with holy horror when she thinks it was once her home."[12] Bond Street, where the Warners had visited the Wards, was now the site of Flynn's "disreputable" bar.[13] In the 1890's, one venerable octogenarian, a contemporary of Susan Warner, "pined once more to see the long-ago beautiful place" around St. Mark's, Lafayette Place, and Bond Street. "As her carriage rolled on she contrasted the past with the present; she exclaimed, 'all is dark and changed except the Marble Cemetery; that looks as it used to. I never want to come here again."[14]

The world of fashion that Susan Warner knew passed quickly. Financially crippled or bankrupted by the Panic of 1837 and the six years of national economic hardship that followed, many of the fashionable families, like the Warners, disappeared from the city or at least from its better sections. It was not until the 1850's that full economic prosperity again returned; and by that time, the newly rich and fashionable, who were building their brownstone mansions to the north near Madison Square had little knowledge of—or, for that matter, interest in the customs and manners of an earlier New York.

### III  *Town and Country*

*Queechy*, which Susan began a short while after she returned from her visit to the Putnams, was completed and in print two years later. Like *The Wide, Wide World*, *Queechy* has a relatively simple plot, considering its great length. (Both novels run to more than 350,000 words—far more than the average American novel of the day.) The action is divided largely between New York City and a country village, Queechy, which is clearly based on Canaan, New York. The farm and farmhouse where much of the novel takes place are, like those in *The Wide, Wide World*, based on the Warner property in Canaan.

At the beginning of the novel, a young orphan, Fleda Ringgan, is living with her grandfather on a farm on the outskirts of Queechy. The grandfather is nearly cheated out of his property but his debts are paid and his property saved by a young and wealthy acquaintance from England, Guy Carleton. A short time later, Fleda's grandfather dies, and she is sent to live with her aunt and uncle, Mr. and Mrs. Rolf Rossitur, in France. Sometime later, her uncle, because of financial difficulties, is forced to leave France and bring his family to New York, where they are able to live in at least comfortable, if less elegant, circumstances, Mr. Rossitur's financial difficulties increase, and finally his family has to leave New York and move to the Ringgan farm in Queechy, where they hope to make a living as farmers. The Rossiturs know little about farming, however; and it is only through Fleda's help and advice that they are able to get by. Meanwhile, many of the Rossitur's wealthy and fashionable friends—including Dr. Gregory and the Evelyn family—become Fleda's friends, and a large portion of the book concerns her visits to them.

The Rossiturs' financial difficulties increase; and, like Fleda's grandfather, they are nearly cheated out of all their possessions. Dr. Gregory holds the title to the property, however, and this fact, together with Fleda's careful management, at least assures them of a home. In the end, however, it is only the timely intervention of Fleda and Guy Carleton that saves the Rossiturs from absolute ruin. At the end of the novel, Fleda and Carleton are married and move to his family home in England.

### IV   An Aristocracy of Manners

Susan's primary object in *Queechy* was to outline the distinction between an aristocracy of virtue and manners (represented by her heroine) and an aristocracy of wealth and birth. Like *The Wide, Wide World*, *Queechy* is a didactic novel; and just as the earlier book concerns certain religious and spiritual values, the second concerns ideal social values and manners.

*Queechy*'s New York geography is the sort that a young lady like Susan, growing up in fashionable society, would have known in the 1830's. The customs, the general pattern of life, are also those of upper-class life in that decade. What is perhaps less obvious, the novel's idealization of an aristocracy of manners—at the expense of aristocracies of birth and wealth—also firmly ties the book to that era. As Stow Persons has shown, the aristocracy of manners was still widely idealized in this country in the late nineteenth and early twentieth centuries—but never as intensely or universally as in the earlier decades.[15]

The aristocracy of manners, which Susan made the subject of her novel, was a reaction to two social forces: Jacksonian democracy and the unprecedented great national wealth that followed the completion of the Erie Canal in 1825. It was, of course, New York which, above all, benefited from the canal, and the result was a newly wealthy class of merchants and professionals, few of whom had the ancestral credentials of the city's old Dutch and English aristocracies. But what these newly rich men and their families lacked in genealogies, they made up in a desire for social polish and the veneer of good manners. A man's behavior as well as his money could distinguish him from the rest of the populace.

The Jacksonian era marks the entrance of the common man into fields, notably politics, from which he had traditionally been excluded; but, paradoxically, it also marks a new popular attention to the value of aristocracies, especially their traditional support of mannered and cultured experience. Undoubtedly, this was in part a reflexive defense by people who saw their cultivated lives and traditional values scorned by a large and, politically, newly powerful frontier population. The new attention to aristocracies and their value was in theory, however, heavily democratic. Few people were willing to defend privilege, especially the traditional rights of wealth and birth; but many were willing to defend the traditional aristocratic values of cultivated manners and moral ideals. The frontier argued for practical and simple values; the East or at least Whigs like Susan and her father responded by insisting on the importance of traditional morals and manners. These might be difficult to cultivate and practice, but they were the marks of the lady or gentleman—the true aristocrat, the person deserving, it was said, universal respect.

Since wealth and birth were no longer used to define the aristocrat, a pauper could, at least theoretically, be as much an aristocrat in this country as could a great landholder, and, in fact, this was insisted upon by Americans who defended aristocratic values. "In no country is it more important to cultivate good manners, than in our own," insisted the authoress of *The Young Lady's Friend* in 1838; a lady might very well be a seamstress; for it was, after all, manners and not wealth or occupation that determined social rank.[16] Catharine Maria Sedgwick spoke for her age when she said that in a country "where all are born to equal rights," only manners could be used to distinguish one class from another. Manners, she explained, are "the expressions of [people's] dispositions and affections. . . . the outward signs of the qualities of [their] minds and hearts."[17] In short, manners were signs of one's moral character. "Manners," Stow Persons has said, "were indeed the outer forms of inner reality"—or so it was argued—"and in them the tone and spirit of social relations were fully realized."[18]

Of special significance, because of its effect on characterization in *Queechy*, is the era's sense of ideal behavior in women. As Mrs. John Farrar wrote in her etiquette book for young girls, the woman who was modest, refined, and considerate was a lady; but "the person who is bold, coarse, vociferous, and inattentive to the rights and feelings of others, is a vulgar woman, let her possessions be ever so great, and her way of living ever so genteel."[19] Miss Sedgwick, who was probably the most widely read and influential authority on manners, insisted that girls should "express in [their] manners that inner purity, delicacy and refinement which is the charm of [their] sex, and essential to a woman."[20]

## V  *Christian Character*

Fleda Ringgan is the novel's ideal aristocrat, a person characterized by perfect manners rather than wealth, dress, ancestry, or social influence. Although she has spent most of her childhood in the country and far from the world of fashionable life, she possesses, says Guy Carleton, a "high breeding," which "can neither be given nor bequeathed; and we can not entail it."[21] Although this "high breeding" could be taught, Carleton says, it is seldom learned and by no means the exclusive possession of fashionable society. Fleda is quiet, modest, selfless, and disinterested—characteristics that, it is soon clear, are the direct outgrowth of her moral principles and Christian beliefs. She has, above all, an absolute trust in God and believes, like Ellen Montgomery, that misfortune has been intended by God in some way for her benefit. Manners and morality are not relative matters, dependent on particular circumstances: they are unchanging and absolute, knowable to all who will study the Scriptures and submit themselves to divine authority.

Like Fleda, her grandfather and his sister possess the ideal qualities and manners that define the Christian. They may lack "*polish* of manner"; but they possess "sterling sense," "good feeling," "true hearty hospitality," and "dignified courtesy."[22] Fleda and her grandfather are both poor; but neither cares "a jot for the want of elegancies which one [despises], and the other if she [has] ever known [has] well nigh forgotten."[23]

The world is viewed as the corrupting influence—as indeed it invariably is seen in the writings of evangelical Christianity. Fleda prays that she may "be kept pure from the world's contact"; and Carleton believes it would be almost better for Fleda to die than that "self-interest should sharpen the eye, and the lines of diplomacy write themselves on that fair brow."[24] Fleda would much less prefer to live among fashionable people than to be in Queechy, "among the rough things of life, where she [can] do so much to smooth them for others and her own spirit [can] grow to a polish it [would] never gain in the regions of ease and pleasure."[25] Her reward is presumably a moral fulfillment or satisfaction, but, contrary (of course) to the author's intention, this reward appears to be a self-justified conceit. Indeed, as the following passage demonstrates, Fleda's self-satisfaction with her good deeds is, like the language with which it is described, extraordinarily vulgar and disagreeable:

Anything more white and spirit-looking, and more spirit-like, in its purity and peacefulness, [than Fleda] surely did not walk that night. There was music in her ear, and abroad in the star-light, more ethereal than Ariel's , but she knew where it came from; it was the chimes of her heart that were ringing; and never a happier peal, nor never had the mental atmosphere been more clear for their sounding. Thankfulness,—that was the oftenest note,—swelling thankfulness for her success,—joy, for herself and for the dear ones at home,—generous delight at having been the instrument of their relief,—the harmonies of pure affections, without any grating now,—the hope, well grounded she thought, of improvement in her uncle and better times for them all,—a childlike peace that was at rest with itself and the world,—these were mingling and interchanging their music, and again and again in the midst of all, faith rang the last chime in heaven.[26]

It would be a mistake to judge the book by passages like this—in fact there are, mercifully, few of them—but in the novel's didactic scheme they are supremely important, providing a justification for Fleda's disinterestedness and her sacrifices.

## VI  *Artificial Aristocracies*

Fleda's uncle, Mr. Rossitur, is a man of considerable talent, learning, and wealth, who has made his life as cultured and as socially cultivated as his means have permitted. He is "not extravagant in his pleasures, nor silly in his ostentation, but [leads], like a gentleman, as worthy and rational a life as a man can lead who lives only to himself, with no further thought than to enjoy the passing hours."[27] As long as he is among people as wealthy and cultured as he, Mr. Rossitur is a considerate and admirable man, but reduced to the poverty of life in Queechy, he becomes disagreeable, hating the local people and himself for his economic disgrace. Ellen is able to accommodate herself to any situation—although she is always aware of a moral superiority in herself—but Mr. Rossitur is fit only for the life to which his wealth has accustomed him. The Yankees in Queechy immediately recognize his shortcomings as a farmer and dislike him for his pretensions. He, on the other hand, refuses to accommodate himself either to his new life or to the customs of his neighbors. Particularly disagreeable to him is the fact that many of the local Yankees are related to him by marriage and so claim the respect due a kinsman. I am in "a nest of cousins," he cries in disgust, "and I had rather be in a nest of rooks. I wonder if I shall be expected to ask my ploughman to dinner! Every second man is a cousin, and the rest are uncles."[28]

The New York City geography that Susan Warner uses in chapters involving the Rossiturs and their friends tells much about their values and the author's attitudes toward them. The Rossiturs live in a "snug handsome American house"—a townhouse on State Street in the oldest part of the city.[29] Dr. Gregory has an "old house in Bleecker Street,"[30] and her friends, the Evelyns, live in rather elegant surroundings on Fourteenth Street. Each address had special significance to nineteenth-century American readers. The Rossiturs are of good family but, because of their recent economic troubles, have no great wealth; and so they live in an older, still fashionable section of the city, where a home cost less than in the newer sections like Gramercy Park. Bleecker Street was, as we have noted, one of the best addresses in the city and the expected place for a man like Dr. Gregory to live—a man, that is, of substantial wealth and a man as concerned with good books and fine manners as with good society. Dr. Gregory may have been patterned on the Warners' good friend Dr. John Wakefield Francis, but the Bleecker Street house described in the novel was almost certainly drawn after the home of the Reverend Thomas Skinner, at which Susan was a frequent guest. In fact, Susan was a house guest there immediately after her visit to the Putnams and just before she began writing her second novel; and her choice of this house as a setting for her book may well have resulted from this occasion.

The choice of Fourteenth Street as the Evelyns' address is also significant. The street and adjacent Union Square had been laid out in the 1830s, and the new homes there, all richly appointed, were occupied by newly rich merchants and their families, people eager to establish good social credentials. There were, of course, old families here as well—including the elder Henry James and his family—yet it was exactly the place where one might encounter people like the Evelyns, thriving on an assumed, but by no means assured, social superiority.

Dr. Gregory is one of Susan Warner's ideal figures, but it is his learning, manners, books, and conversation for which he is respected. The Decatur family, who are mentioned briefly, appear to be the same sort of people, more interested in learning than in fashion. They hold *conversazioni* at which the guests are expected to speak German or French—the sort of gathering which Susan, though not the Evelyns, would welcome. (It was just such New York *conversazioni* and the cultural pretensions they suggested that James Fenimore Cooper satirized in *Home As Found*.)

Among the New Yorkers, Dr. Gregory and the Decaturs are ideal figures, and Mr. Rossitur is agreeable as long as he is surrounded by people who share his interests. But among the Evelyns Fleda finds little to admire or approve. The youngest of the three daughters, Edith, is sensible and "sober," but her older sisters, Constance and Florence, and their mother concern themselves mainly with fashion and ways of spending their merchant-father's newly acquired fortune. To Fleda, their interests are frivolous and transitory. One of their friends argues that women have little need for reading, and it is clear that the Evelyn daughters are in agreement.[31] There is nothing in the Evelyns' society to interest Fleda, and she concludes that she would far rather be isolated in Queechy than be entertained by all the fashionable rich of New York.

Incidentally, a few, unfortunately brief passages set this New York in a larger social context—passages that describe Chatham Square and sections of Chelsea. These areas, inhabited by immigrants and the poor, were known to people like the Warners more through rumor than experience. One imagines that Susan Warner knew these areas only because of her charitable work in the Mercer Street Church. The distinction between the poor and the rich sections of New York was clear-cut a century ago; and Fleda knows that once she has crossed into the Chelsea area—which is necessary at one point for her to do—there is little chance that she will meet anyone she knows.[32] Geography, once again, reflects character and social position.

## VII   *The Yankees*

Fleda, after a visit to New York, finds herself "half coming to the conclusion that her place henceforth was only at [Queechy] and that the world and she had nothing to do with each other."[33] On the surface, it is an unexpected conclusion for one of Susan's heroines; the author herself, as we have seen, cared little for Canaan and its rural customs. In fact, a closer examination of the book suggests that it is merely the secluded life at Queechy, not the people who live there, that Fleda prefers. She is able to deal with the people there and is well liked—and, therefore, succeeds in managing the farm, after her uncle, who openly disdains his workers and other local residents, has failed. Nonetheless, she considers herself very much their social and moral superior, an opinion that the author clearly shares. To cite one minor but otherwise typical example, Fleda discovers that a local sawmill has "a picturesque charm for her, where the country people [see] nothing but business and a place fit for it. Their hands grow hard where her mind [is] refining. Where they [make] dollars and cents, she [is] growing rich in stores of thought and associations of beauty."[34] At another point, Fleda is unable to avoid having dinner at a local farmhouse where conditions—to her "unspeakable horror"—are not very sanitary. "A temporary locked-jaw would have been felt a blessing," the author comments.[35]

Susan's attitude toward New England life and customs is the same in *Queechy* as in *The Wide, Wide World*; but although it is clear that she dislikes rural, uneducated Yankees—or at best is amused by them, she is able to render New England local color with exceptional detail and precision. Local manners and customs, modes of dress, types of houses, social gatherings, colloquial expressions, and rhythms of speech are all carefully recorded. Just as Aunt Fortune's "bee" is one of the best episodes in *The Wide, Wide World*, so are the quilting bee, the donation party for the minister, and the sugaring-off party among the best things in *Queechy*. As a record of New England life, the novel is of considerable historical as well as literary value.

Susan deals with local color in *Queechy* in the same manner that she employed in *The Wide, Wide World*. The deatils of rural New

England life are reported with photographic precision, but there is always a moral or social commentator present—usually Fleda—to signal the author's disapproval of the customs she so carefully records. Every opportunity is taken to underscore the Yankees' provinciality, their poor manners, moral weaknesses, and lack of education. One Yankee farmwife, who has earlier noted that she would "rather have a good dish o' bread and 'lasses" than roast meat for dinner, tells Fleda,

"I want to know what kind of a place New York is, now . . . . I s'pose it's pretty big, ain't it?"
Fleda replied that it was.
"I shouldn't wonder if it was a'most as far as from here to Queechy Run, now, ain't it?"
The distance mentioned being somewhere about one-eighth of New York's longest diameter, Fleda answered that it was quite as far.
"I s'pose there's plenty o' mighty rich folks there, ain't there?"
"Plenty, I believe," said Fleda.
"I should hate to live in it awfully!" was the old woman's conclusion.

Given her social perspective and sense of class, it is not surprising that although Susan could record local color accurately and vividly, she could not do so with complete sympathy. In this respect, she was like Harriet Beecher Stowe whose novels of New England life often take a superior and patronizing attitude toward their materials. It was the special achievement of Sarah Orne Jewett, a generation later, to deal with Yankee customs and manners for their intrinsic value, rather than as foils or contrasts to other values or ideals.

## VIII   *Reception*

*Queechy* sold exceptionally well in its day; and although never as popular as *The Wide, Wide World*, it remained in print throughout the century and continued to receive good critical notices. In 1853, the *North British Review* called it "a book without parallel, except in the 'Wide Wide World,' [sic]"[36] and as late as 1886 a critic in *The Nineteenth Century* claimed that "Fleda in *Queechy* is second only, if she is not equal, as a literary study, to Little Nell in [Charles Dickens's] *The Old Curiosity Shop*."[37] Writing to Mary Russell Mitford, Elizabeth Barrett Browning asked if she had "read 'Queechy,' the American book—novel—by Elizabeth Wetherell [the pseudonym under which the book was published]? I think it very clever and characteristic. Mrs. Beecher Stowe [sic] scarcely exceeds it, after all the trumpets." High praise indeed, since at this time Mrs. Stowe's *Uncle Tom's Cabin* had made her one of the most respected authors in the world.[38]

Sales in both England and America were impressive. Like *The Wide, Wide World*, *Queechy* was also published in England—in pirated editions, however, that paid the author no royalties. One English publisher, Routledge's, alone sold substantially more than a hundred thousand copies. Because publishing records have been lost and scattered, it is impossible to determine what the book's total sales were during the half century it remained in print. No one doubted, however, that the book, while never approaching the unprecedented popularity of *The Wide, Wide World*, was among the great best sellers of the day. Its popularity is attested by the fact that one English railway bookstall alone is reported to have sold ten thousand copies.

*Queechy's* popularity must be partially attributed to the reputation that *The Wide, Wide World* had established for its author. The success of that first novel was so obvious a selling point for her later works that most of them were issued as "by the author of *The Wide, Wide World*." The pseudonym "Elizabeth Wetherell," which Susan used when she began to publish, was soon omitted, and the author's real name seldom appeared. Even Anna's *Dollars and Cents* in a reprint edition carried on its cover the legend, "BY THE AUTHOR OF THE WIDE WIDE WORLD."[39]

It would be, no doubt, an error to attribute *Queechy's* success solely to its predecessor's reputation. A novel's popular success may very well promote, but can not guarantee, a good reception for its successors—as Mrs. Stowe discovered when she followed *Uncle Tom's Cabin* (1851 - 52) with *Dred, A Tale of the Dismal Swamp* (1857), a book which received polite notices in the journals but the sales of which were far below expectations. Maria Cummins's *The Lamplighter* (1854) was a best seller, but its successors—*Mable Vaughan* (1857), *El Fureidis* (1860), and *Haunted Hearts* (1864)—received progressively less attention and were soon forgotten. Surely *Queechy* needed more than a famous predecessor to insure its success.

*The Wide, Wide World* appealed directly to the evangelical spirit of the age; it reflected the dominant religious sensibility of the day. *Queechy* in turn appealed to a social temper that, having rejected most of the traditional insignia of class as undemocratic, still viewed society in terms of morals and manners.

Undoubtedly, these books were successful partly because they appealed directly to women. If both books have heroes—John Humphreys and Guy Carleton, respectively—they remain shadowy figures, little characterized. It is the heroines, Ellen Montgomery and Fleda Ringgan, with which the author and her readers were most concerned. The male worlds of business and money-getting clearly have a primary effect on the novels; both books begin with economic failures that adversely effect the heroines' lives. But Susan Warner, and presumably her readers, were less interested in what caused these economic downfalls—they are never explained—than in their effect on Fleda and Ellen. *The Wide, Wide World* and *Queechy* are *domestic* novels; their settings are the home and the family, realms traditionally reserved for, or controlled by, women.

## IX   *My Father's Keeper*

*The Hills of the Shatemuc* (1856), Susan's third novel, was one of the few she wrote centered on a hero rather than a heroine. As if to underscore the fact that her first two novels were popular partly because they dealt with women, *The Hills of the Shatemuc*, despite good publicity and some good reviews, sold poorly—so poorly in fact that it was soon forgotten and generally overlooked in later studies of her life and works.

The book is based on the youth and early manhood of the author's father, and many of the details were taken directly from old family letters. The setting is not Canaan, however; and this may be the book's most significant fault. The Canaan setting had offered rich local-color materials for *Queechy* and *The Wide, Wide World*, but there are few regional details in *The Hills of the Shatemuc*. Nominally, the setting is the Hudson and the hills around it, but descriptions are vague, with little sense of local customs and life. There are occasionally good descriptions of the poorer sections of New York but nothing to match those in *Queechy*. Although Susan utilized interesting historical and family information for her plot, she failed to surround it with the rich sense of time and place that is characteristic of her earlier books.

The narrative begins at the farm of Orphah Landholm, a moderately prosperous farmer who has mortgaged his property to a

New Yorker, Mr. Haye. Haye sends his daughter Rose and niece Elizabeth Cadwallader to spend summer months at the farm. Elizabeth is impressed by Landholm's son Winthrop and especially by his ambition, shared by his older brother Rufus, to get an education and improve his position in life. Winthrop's ambitions are eventually fulfilled—although his brother's are not—and he later studies law in New York and is admitted to the bar. After Mrs. Landholm's death, Haye forecloses the mortgage, and Mr. Landholm is forced to go west to see if his fortune will be any better there. Meanwhile, Elizabeth, unknown to Haye, purchases the Landholm farm; and after Haye's death a short while later—it appears that he has died insolvent, bankrupt or very nearly so—she moves to the farm and invites Rose to come and live with her. Winthrop visits them there, and it is suggested, at the end of the book, that eventually Elizabeth will marry him.

It is difficult to extricate the plot's historical base from its fictional development. The early chapters, dealing with the Landholm farm and Winthrop's and Rufus's ambitions, are clearly biographical; it is, of course, the Warner farm that is being described, and Winthrop Landholm is based on the author's father. Rufus Landholm is clearly drawn after Thomas Warner, Henry Warner's brother; this parallel has been conclusively demonstrated by Mabel Baker in her study of the Warner family.[40] It is somewhat more difficult to find originals for Elizabeth, Mr. Haye, and his daughter Rose; indeed, the whole episode of the mortgage seems at first glance fictional—surprisingly so, since the rest of the novel is such a precise transcription of Warner family history. In fact, the episode may have been suggested by, if not entirely based on, circumstances involving the Warners' farm in Brooklyn. If Elizabeth is, to a degree, based on the author's mother—and there are decided similarities in personality—then conceivably Elizabeth's guardian, Mr. Haye, may be based on Anna Bartlett's stepfather, Cornelius Bogert. In fact, Bogert owned a substantial share of the Warners' farm in Brooklyn. Susan Warner had very fond childhood memories of the Bogerts and their hospitality, but a division apparently developed between the two families later. Bogert—unlike Mr. Haye in the novel—died a very wealthy man; yet he left nothing to the Warners, a fact that is even more astonishing in view of his earlier generosity to them.[41] The mortgage episode in *The Hills of the Shatemuc* is fictional, but the personal and economic tensions between the Landholms and the Hayes may reflect similar tensions between the Bogerts and the Warners.

## X  *The Way Down*

*The Hills of the Shatemuc* is interesting to the student of Susan Warner's work because of its biographical significance—but this is its only real value. As a literary work, it is among the author's least successful. It lacks, as noted above, a firm sense of time and place—the most substantial literary achievements of her earlier fiction. Perhaps the problems inherent in dealing with a central hero instead of heroine made this inevitable. Winthrop's world of business and law was something Susan Warner knew only by rumor.

The diction is pale, uninspired; even the descriptions of the hills that give the novel its title are ordinary and flat:

The mountains and the northern sky and clouds were floating as it were in a warm flush of light—it was upon the clouds, and through the air, and upon the mountains' sides,—so fair, so clear, but beyond that, so rich in its glowing profusion of beauty, that eyes and tongue were stayed,—the one from leaving the subject, the other from touching it.[42]

Not even the convoluted grammar can disguise the flat and uninspired language, nor the peculiar vulgarity of the final image.

*The Hills of the Shatemuc* was written under self-imposed pressure, the author making herself write a certain number of pages each day. Had it been written in less haste, it might well have been a better book; but it is unlikely that the central problem—the fact that she was dealing with a hero rather than a heroine—could ever have been resolved. The author simply did not have the experience or the imaginative ability to deal satisfactorily with the matter. Less haste might also have improved the novel's weak diction—but not the vague and faulty characterization of the hero. The answer here lies in the narrowness of the author's world.

Initially, *The Hills of the Shatemuc* was enormously popular; ten thousand copies, it is said, were sold on the first day—an unprecedented figure. But the enthusiasm soon waned; and while *The Wide, Wide World* and *Queechy* continued to sell, the sales for *The Hills of the Shatemuc* stopped. "All the promise contained in [the author's] earlier works. . . ," wrote a critic in the *Athenaeum*, "appears to have evaporated,—the power of exciting the reader's interest is gone,—there is no knowledge to make up for the romance that is lost,—and there is no clearness of intention, nor truth of experience, to give value to the didactic portions."[43] "Our American romancers," he concluded, "after their first rush of success, seem to be falling flat as yesterday's champagne."[44] And the novelist Charles Kingsley, noting the novel's interminable dialogues, dismissed it as "*The Hills of the Chattermuch.*"[45]

CHAPTER 4

# My Sister's Keeper

B Y the way what do you think of spirits meeting? Does not mine embrace yours? Do I not *feel* the breath of love from your lips?
—Susan Warner in a letter to her sister, April, 1848[1]

## I Anna

Anna Warner was nearly as prolific a writer as her sister, but few of her works have literary value, and those that still can interest literary historians and critics are, by and large, imitations of her sister's writings. Anna is still remembered for her novel *Dollars and Cents* (1852), a best seller in its day; her co-authorship of *Say and Seal* (1860), a novel of considerable interest in the history of New England local color; and several of her hymns, of which the best known are "I Would See Jesus" and "Jesus Loves Me."[2] She was also known in her day as the author of many children's books, including *Robinson Crusoe's Farmyard* (1848) and various books in a series entitled Ellen Montgomery's Bookshelf, issued between 1853 and 1859. She wrote religious and didactic tales and tracts and edited several volumes of hymns. Together with her sister, she worked on a series of books, collectively entitled The Word, which interpreted the Bible for young readers. She was also the author of books on gardening. (In fact, *Gardening By Myself* (1872) was recently reissued in a new edition and is the only one of her books now in print.) She wrote biographies of her sister, of the Reverend George Ainslie, and of James and Caroline Phelps Stokes.

The Stokes biography, *Some Memories of James and Caroline Phelps Stokes* (1892), is potentially of much value to social historians, but copies are difficult to locate—only a hundred were printed—and it has been generally overlooked. The Stokes family was of much social and religious influence in nineteenth-century New York. Mrs. Stokes's father was Anson G. Phelps, a wealthy

73

merchant who financially backed the great revivalist preacher Charles Grandison Finney during his ministry in New York. The Stokes family were also major supporters of Thomas Harvey Skinner and were among the founders of the Mercer Street Presbyterian Church. Anna's biography of Mr. Stokes and his wife is a substantial volume of 460 pages, consisting largely of letters and diaries which document the close ties between New York's wealthy merchant and professional classes and the rise of evangelical Presbyterianism.[3]

It was through their mutual interest in the Mercer Street Presbyterian Church that Anna was acquainted with Mr. and Mrs. Stokes. Many years later, a daughter, Olivia E. Phelps Stokes, vividly remembered as a child seeing Anna and her sister, "slender and dignified," after the Sunday morning service on Mercer Street.[4] Throughout her life, she remained very much in awe of the sisters and finally wrote and published a tribute to them—a curious collection of anecdotes, local history, genealogical tables, and letters—entitled *Letters and Memories of Susan and Anna Bartlett Warner* (1925).

## II  *Sugarplums*

Much of Anna's "fiction" is in fact closely autobiographical. Unlike her sister, she did not possess the imaginative ability to transform personal experience into fiction. *The Wide, Wide World, Queechy,* and *Dollars and Cents* concern families that have lost their money and social prestige; and all three were suggested by the Warners' personal misfortunes. But while Susan was able to transform those materials into fiction, having an integrous life of its own, Anna transcribed her families' experiences virtually diary-fashion, changing few pertinent details except names and a few incidental facts. So much of her book is demonstrably auto-biographical—a point-by-point record of actual events—that *Dollars and Cents* can hardly be called fiction at all.

Anna's general inability or disinterest in transforming experience into fiction is evident in the three "Sybil and Chryssa" volumes that she contributed to Ellen Montgomery's Bookshelf, a series of books that supposedly belonged to Miss Alice—in *The Wide, Wide World*—and which Ellen Montgomery especially liked. *Mr. Rutherford's Children* (1853) was the first to be published, followed shortly by *Carl Krinken: His Christmas Stocking* (1853). (This was the most popular volume in the series, and a new illustrated edition was published as late as 1911.) In 1854, a second volume of *Mr. Ruther-*

*ford's Children* was issued. *Casper* was published in 1856; *Hard Maple*, in 1859. A sequel to *Mr. Rutherford's Children, Happy Days, or Holly Farm* concluded the series. The two volumes of *Mr. Rutherford's Children* and *Happy Days* comprise the Sybil and Chryssa series, all of which were closely based on Anna's childhood memories. Contrary to some accounts, incidentally, Anna wrote *all* the volumes in Ellen Montgomery's Bookshelf except *Carl Krinken*, which was written by her sister.[5]

The three Sybil and Chryssa books concern the Rutherford family—Sybil and Chryssa and their aunt and uncle, Mr. and Mrs. Rutherford. None of the three has more than minimal connective plot; each consists of a series of loosely related episodes. The first volume is set at the Rutherford farm, Rose Hill, and involves—in no particular order—such things as birthdays, pet cats, and visits to the girls' grandmother. The second volume is set in a city—presumably New York, although this is never explicitly stated—where Sybil, Chryssa, and their guardians, are spending the winter. The book details their social visits, shopping expeditions, preparations for and celebration of Christmas. In the third volume, the Rutherfords visit a farm.

Characterization in these books is as minimal as their plots. Mr. and Mrs. Rutherford, aside from their basic goodness and generosity, are virtually uncharacterized. Sybil and Chryssa are presented as ideal children: cheerful, honest, generous, and respectful toward their elders. The children's lives are ones of unalloyed sweetness. While these books are simple—and, the modern reader might argue, simpleminded—to the point of monotony, their objective is serious. They are, after all, didactic tales for children, for whom they provide ideal models of behavior. The books teach good manners and morals by offering sketches of well-mannered, virtuous children. In this respect, the books are similar to *Queechy* and *The Wide, Wide World*, but because of their watery plots and diluted characterizations, the Sybil and Chryssa books are far less effective or convincing in their didacticism.

The following passage from the first volume is representative of the books' didactic method:

"But Chryssa if Betsy offers us any candy to-day, let's not take it." [said Sybil]

"Why?" said Chryssa—"I like that candy very much,—Betsy gave me some twice, and I eat [sic] it all up. It tasted just like cloves. I never saw such candy anywhere else; why shouldn't we take it?"

"Because," said Sybil, "Betsy keeps it to sell, and it doesn't seem right for us to eat it. I know it's very good, but she might get a penny for every stick she gives us; and she is poor."

"Well if that's all," said Chryssa, "I'll give her a penny for it too. I would have asked Aunt Esther for one if you'd told me."

"But Betsy wouldn't let us pay for it," said Sybil,—"I'm sure she wouldn't. She's always very glad to give it to us, but then I don't think we ought to take it."

"Well I won't then," said Chryssa. . . .[6]

Sybil and Chryssa's moral dilemmas are never more trying or subtle than this. Ellen Montgomery is confronted with a cruel and unsympathetic world, and Fleda Ringgan has to save the Rossitur family from bankruptcy, but Sybil and Chryssa never have to bother themselves with difficulties more severe than whether or not to accept Betsy's penny candy.

The Sybil and Chryssa books, as mentioned above, are based on Anna's memories of her childhood: the farm in Brooklyn and the Bogert estate at Jamaica (*Mr. Rutherford's Children*, I), winters in New York hotels before the Broome Street and St. Mark's Place houses were purchased (*Mr. Rutherford's Children*, II), and visits to the Warner homestead in Canaan (*Happy Days*). Mr. and Mrs. Rutherford are based on Henry Whiting Warner and Aunt Fanny; Sybil and Chryssa, on the author and her sister. Anyone who knows the Warners' biographies—notably as outlined by Anna in her book about her sister—can recognize the broad similarities between the books and the author's life.

The books are cluttered with details—including quite explicit descriptions of furnishings, wallpaper, and landscapes—that contribute nothing to the stories nor to their didactic purposes; one assumes that these details are, like the stories themselves, more the product of memory than imagination. The Sybil and Chryssa books have an interest for anyone curious about the Warners' childhood; but because of their haphazard organization and shallow characterizations, they are, like so many of Anna's publications, of little interest as literature.

### III   *Bankruptcy, Again*

*Dollars and Cents* or *Glen Luna*, as it was titled in England, was Anna's first and most popular novel. The story concerns a wealthy Philadelphia family, the Howards, who lose their money and consequently their social standing, largely because of the father's unfortunate financial speculations. Mr. Howard; his daughters, Kate and Gracie (the book's narrator); their stepmother; and his ward, Stephanie Holbrook, leave Philadelphia and move to Glen Luna—"A large property," according to a real estate advertisement, "on the banks of Lake Luna,—consisting of meadow, farm, and woodland—splendid sites for country-seats, unrivalled water-power, &c., &c., &c."[7] Mr. Howard feels certain that he will be able to develop his new property as a resort and location for summer houses. The thousand acres that comprise Glen Luna, he claims, will someday make his fortune. Mrs. Howard is somewhat less sanguine about his plans and ambitions, however; but dutiful wife that she is, she submits to his judgment and the judgment of his brother Ned, who is certain that ". . . the purchase money could be doubled in no time. . . ."[8]

Far from making Mr. Howard's fortune, Glen Luna eventually reduces him to abject poverty. Like many American real estate speculations of the time, Mr. Howard's proposed real estate development comes to nothing more than maps, plans, and fancy drawings. Among other difficulties, a neighbor burns the Howards' sawmill because it competes with his own. Lengthy and expensive legal proceedings follow: "Suits and crosssuits, and pleas and bills and demurrers,—money to be paid for all. Dollars here for witnesses, and there for a journey to some distant court; and again for a speech which Mr. Howard said wasn't worth a pin. The war of poor against rich injustice."[9] Stephanie, meanwhile, marries and leaves home. (At no point, incidentally, does she play any large role in the novel; she could easily have been omitted without materially damaging the story.)

The Howards' troubles increase, and they are at last forced to sacrifice all but a few pieces of furniture. Meanwhile, most of their old friends in Philadelphia ignore them. Even though some of these former friends establish country estates in the neighborhood of Glen Luna, the Howards find friends only among the year-round country people. Ultimately, even they, or at least many of them, socially cut the Howards. "We were gradually learning to do without more things than money," says Gracie,"—people fell off from us right and left; and the same persons who two or three years before had invited us constantly to their houses, now asked us once in the season, or not at all."[10] When everything seems hopeless—except to the Howards, for no matter what happens to them, they refuse to despair—Mr. Howard is offered a professorship in Greek at a college which is to be established nearby, and Kate marries a man who is as virtuous and good as she.

## IV  *Fiction and Autobiography*

Aside from the conclusion of the novel, *Dollars and Cents* is essentially a chronicle of the Warners' lives from the time their father purchased Constitution Island until the royalties from their books gave the family a small degree of economic security. For New York, Anna substituted Philadelphia; the Warner home on the Hudsom became the Howard home on Lake Luna; Constitution Island became the Lake Luna property; Mr. Warner, Susan, Anna, Aunt Fanny, and Uncle Thomas Warner became, respectively, Mr. Howard, Kate, Gracie, the stepmother, and Uncle Ned Howard. Indeed Anna's characterization of her father (in her biography of her sister) as a man who could not "even *imagine* a breach of honor"—and who, therefore, could not predict his own unjust treatment in the hands of his neighbors and the courts—might well stand as an apt summary of Mr. Howard's character.[11]

The source of many of the Warners' legal difficulties and burdensome expenses was a dam that the Warners had built and that a neighbor had destroyed because it was, he said, "a nuisance."[12] "There followed," wrote Anna, "years of litigation; it seems to me I grew up on it; witnesses, papers, trials, suits; and these things *cost.* . . . But meanwhile the river flowed in and out, in and out, over our poor meadows, with all the dollars spent on them sinking rapidly beyond our reach."[13] In the novel, the neighbor destroys a sawmill rather than a dam, but the end result is the same: legal difficulties and poverty. Finally, just as in the novel, the Howards are forced to sacrifice nearly all their furniture, so did the Warners have to give up theirs.[14]

Anna changed the autobiographical record substantially only at the end of the book; her father never became a professor of Greek, of course, and her sister never married. But Anna, no doubt, would have thought it only just if things had worked out this way. Her father did consider himself a serious student of Greek and generally carried with him a volume in Greek to read and translate whenever an opportunity presented itself. Furthermore, by concluding the novel with Kate's marriage, Anna was in effect awarding her sister what the Warners clearly felt was deserved but had been denied because of the family's misfortunes. In fact, as we noted earlier, if the family had remained as wealthy and socially prominent as they were when Susan was a young woman, it is almost certain that she—or at least her wealth and social prestige—would have attracted a husband as ideal as the one described by Anna in *Dollars and Cents*.

## V  *Manners*

Like the Sybil and Chryssa books, *Dollars and Cents* is interesting primarily because of its biographical origins. As a literary work, it has little to recommend it and, in fact, fails in exactly those things in which *Queechy* and *The Wide, Wide World* succeed. In the first place, it does not develop any sustained or firm sense of local time and place—any sustained sense, that is, of local color. Occasional use is made of "local characters," and an even more occasional use is made of provincial dialect, but there is no highly developed image of rural life and customs such as is found in *Queechy* and *The Wide, Wide World*.

Anna not only lacked—or at least failed to demonstrate—an ability like her sister's fully to detail and realize a particular region, but she also apparently lacked an ability to suggest variations and shades in character. Here, as in her other books, characters are flat and thin, and little aside from their names or social position distinguishes them. Finally, Susan's intensely moral and religious view of experience is largely missing here, so the book lacks the intensity and earnestness that marks the other novels. Beside *The Wide, Wide World* and *Queechy*, *Dollars and Cents* seems pale and weak, little more than a thinly disguised chronicle of the difficulties that the Warners faced.

However, some passages in the novel—it is impossible to tell whether they are purely fictional or biographical—indicate that Anna could write better than this work, taken as a whole, suggests. She is, like her sister, successful when she describes or hints at the social nuances that divide one class from another. To select one example, much is made of the fact that Mr. Howard works alongside his men when they are haying, the sort of thing that a gentleman like Mr. Rossitur in *Queechy* would never do.

"But papa," said Kate, "do you think it will have a good effect on the men?"

"Think what will have a good effect?—their cutting the grass instead of themselves?"

"No, no,—but your working with them."

"Yes, a very good effect, for they'll have to do something."

"They won't respect you so much—you needn't think it," said Kate gravely.

"Pshaw!"—said my father,—"well, I shall respect myself a great deal more than if I let those six men do nothing all day. . . ."[15]

Later, Kate finds her father at work without his suitcoat on—which, to her at least, is a major transgression for anyone who would be known as a gentleman:

"Now papa," said Kate, "*do* you think it is well for a gentleman to go about with his coat on his arm?"

"Very well,—when he doesn't want it on his back."

"But papa it looks so—"

"Hum"—said Mr. Howard, "I don't see why one may not follow a country fashion as well as a city fashion—when one is in the country."

"It *isn't* the fashion—that is just it, papa,—you wouldn't see any one else do so."

"I beg your pardon,—if you go over to Daisy Lea this morning I don't doubt you will find Mr. Collingwood and his son making hay in as comfortable gear as I am. To be sure they are 'only farmers.' "

"I don't believe you would ever see Captain De Camp looking so, Mr. Howard," said Stephanie.

"Captain De Camp's epaulettes are a part of himself," said my father a little impatiently, "which happily my coat is not. Come, I don't want to hear any more of this,—if my respectibility lies so near the surface and is so easily got rid of, I can't hope to keep it long, any way."[16]

Later, to correct any misimpression he may have made, Mr. Howard tells Kate that "I make some distinction of time and place, . . . —if I sat in the drawing-room without a coat, you might justly complain of me."[17]

At one point in the novel, Gracie—who, like the other women in her family, can no longer afford to dress in the manner expected of a lady—accepts a ride with some people who were once family friends. Two of the girls in the carriage, neither of whom Gracie has seen for many years, looks at her as if ". . . they had *never* seen a calico dress, nor a tartan shawl, nor probably a straw bonnet in October."[18] Nor can these people believe that Gracie may have business to attend to; for in their world, a lady would never be in a hurry—always there would be someone to take care of things for her. When one of the women in the carriage asks Gracie if she is "in a hurry to get home," another of the passengers looks "as if the question were a conventional absurdity."[19]

However subtle and artificial the distinctions of social class may seem, they are real and absolute: gentlemen do not work beside hired laborers, and ladies are never "in a hurry." For economic reasons, the Howards are forced to dispense with the trappings of social class that distinguished them in the city. The novel concludes that the Howards' loss is, of course, really their gain, for by giving up their social pretensions, they free themselves from a life of shallow, but no less tyrannical, social distinctions. Anna, like her sister, had little but contempt for the aristocracy of fashion. In *Dollars and Cents*, the private domestic life of the Howards appears in every way superior to the public social life that they left behind in the city.

In mid-nineteenth-century America, few families had had any real or enduring financial and social security. There were many families like the Howards—and the Warners. This fact may in large measure explain the novel's popularity. Businessmen failed far more often than they succeeded, and the family with social pretensions lived as often on credit as on the husband's earnings. Anna's rejection of the standards promoted by the aristocracy of fashion and wealth must have been secretly satisfying or welcome even to her readers who enjoyed all the advantages of good social position. After all, it was not wise to put all one's faith in fashion. The woman who read *Dollars and Cents* one week in her fashionably appointed parlor or boudoir might the next week face bankruptcy. Few such women of that time had not witnessed similar falls from social grace among their friends and relatives. The satisfaction that the Howards find in being free from the artificial distinctions of fashionable society must have been secretly satisfying or reassuring even to the wealthiest of the novel's readers.

## VI   *Preaching the Gospel*

*Dollars and Cents* is basically a chronicle of events, and unlike Susan Warner's fiction and Anna's later novels, it is only incidentally didactic. The opposite was true of *My Brother's Keeper* (1855),

Anna's only other long work of fiction, aside from her books for children, published during the 1850s. A reviewer for *Putnam's* thought that "her ideas of religious life [expressed in this book] are so ungenial and aggressive . . . that we hope that in future [sic] she will indulge very sparely in 'serious' writing."[20] *My Brother's Keeper* traces the religious conversion of a young army officer, Thornton Clyde, at the hands of his devout sister Rosalie. Thornton, as the reviewer remarked, "prefers the society of his young friends" to that of his sister, and

When we find how she labors to convert him from his frivolous ways, firing whole volleys of Scripture texts at him every time he makes his appearance, we do not wonder at it, even though they were wadded with sisterly kisses. To be pelted with pious quotations, over your eggs and coffee, and rubbed down every evening with a lecture on your sins, is not the pleasantest kind of entertainment for young men. Thornton Clyde . . . must have been a miracle of brotherly kindness, to put up with such an incessant hail of preachment.[21]

## VII   *Say and Seal*

The preaching and piety in the writings of both Anna and Susan Warner can be, even in their best books, so overwhelming and self-righteous as nearly to obscure or destroy their literary interest—a fact that is acutely evident in *Say and Seal* (1860), the first novel that the sisters wrote together.

As one Warner scholar has demonstrated, "it is not possible to tell . . . which parts [of the novel] are Susan's and which are Anna's."[22] One assumes that the New England local-color passages were contributed by Susan, but the assumption is based solely on the observation that such passages are characteristic of her novels and uncommon in Anna's. Certainly the self-righteous attitudes and religious allegory could have been the work of either sister.

*Say and Seal* is the most important book with which Anna's name is associated; and together with *The Wide, Wide World* and *Queechy,* it belongs among her sister's most substantial achievements. Like those two novels, it is historically significant in the tradition of didactic and religious fiction. It is also important for its use of New England local color; indeed, in this regard it is a far more ambitious novel than any other work by either of the sisters.

Initially, the book was only modestly popular—Susan Warner was, she said, "A little mortified that [it] should not have done greater things"—but it maintained a following of readers over the years; and as late as 1901, a new American edition was issued.[23] Nonetheless, the novel has generally escaped the attention of literary critics and historians and has never received the critical attention it deserves.

The plot is simple and direct. (Indeed, one unfriendly reviewer insisted that the book proceeded "at the slowest possible pace to keep moving at all" and was characterized by "gentle purring dullness."[24]) John Endecott Linden comes to Pattaquasset, a small village—based on Old Saybrook, Connecticut—where he has been hired as the local schoolmaster. He lives at a Mrs. Derrick's, who has a daughter Faith. Soon after his arrival, he makes several enemies—people suspicious of his learning and his apparent lack of religious orthodoxy. The attacks on his character increase, and his life is even threatened, but his students and most of the townspeople, including Faith, remain devoted to him. Under his instruction, Faith, a gentle and obedient girl, is converted to Christianity and goes about doing good works for others. Linden is portrayed, meanwhile, as the perfect or ideal man, without moral flaw. Linden, the reader is told toward the end of the novel, is a divinity student who has only temporarily turned to teaching. He completes his education and returns to Pattaquasset. Faith and he are married and leave for a New Hampshire town where he has been offered a post as the local minister.

The book is essentially a religious allegory and even the smallest details of plot are directed toward this end. Throughout the novel, natural fact is offered as the emblem of spiritual truth. The method is evident in the following passage—the paragraph with which the novel opens:

The street was broad with sidewalks, and wide grass-grown borders, and a spacious track of wheels and horses' feet in the centre. Great elms, which the early settlers planted, waved their pendant branches over the peaceful highway, and gave shelter and nest-room to numerous orioles, killdeer, and robins; putting off their yellow leaves in the autumn, and bearing their winter weight of snow, in seeming quiet assurance that spring would make amends for all. So slept the early settlers in the churchyards.[25]

The parallel between natural fact and spiritual idea is effectively suggested here and provides the appropriate beginning for a novel that is essentially an allegory based on the Christian drama of redemption and salvation. The specific terms of the allegory are taken from Paul's first epistle to the Corinthians in which he wrote that ". . . the head of every man is Christ; and the head of the woman is the man. . . ," and also from his epistle to the Ephesians, in which he wrote, "Wives, submit yourselves unto your own husbands, as unto the Lord. For the husband is the head of the wife, even as Christ is the head of the church: and he is the Savior of the body. Therefore as the church is subject unto Christ, so let the wives be unto their own husbands in every thing."[26] The biblical parallel between the woman's love for, and submission to, her husband and the church's love for, and submission to, Christ was well understood by the Warners' contemporaries, laymen as well as theologians.

*Say and Seal* is obsessively concerned with the details of marriage: the preparations, nature of the ritual, the social and religious implications of marriage, and so forth—but the Warners are concerned with such details only insofar as they have an emblematic significance. Faith's growing desire to submit herself to Linden parallels the church's desire to submit itself to Christ. Faith—the reason for her name is obvious—must learn never to question Linden's will and to do nothing but obey it—and enjoy doing so. The ritual of marriage is, following the prescription of Paul, essentially a metaphor for the union of church and Christ.

Susan had suggested this parallel at the end of *The Wide, Wide World* in Ellen's growing devotion to John Humphreys. *Wych Hazel* (1876), *The Gold of Chickaree* (1876), and *Diana* (1877), among others, also parallel the woman's submission to her husband with the church's or individual's submission to Christ. Salvation, these novels preach, begins with willful submission. "A Christian," says Mr. Linden, "is one who, trusting in Christ as his only Savior, thenceforth obeys Him as his only King."[27]

The allegory at the center of the novel is framed by realistic images of the New England community in which the novel is set. These images contribute to the allegorical purpose, although they are not central to it, by providing contrasts to the ideal and morally perfect nature of Mr. Linden. Collectively, the images provide one of the earliest literary descriptions of a complete New England settlement—the sort of accomplishment for which Sarah Orne Jewett's *The Country of the Pointed Firs* (1896) has long been recognized. Among the citizens of Pattaquasset who are characterized—most of them briefly—are fishermen, farmers, spinsters, housewives, deacons, the parson, the seamstress, the schoolmaster, and the doctor. Subtle distinctions in social rank are diagramed. (". . . the De Staffs never had tea carried round unless when they had company; at the Harrisons' it was never carried round unless they were alone," and ". . . while the De Staffs had the show, the Harrisons always had the reality of precedence in the town."[28]) Even the names of the townspeople evoke a special provincial or New England flavor: Reuben Taylor, Miss Delia Danforth, Charles Twelfth Seacomb and his brother Americus Vespucus Seacomb, Sam Stoutenburgh, and so forth. Characteristic local activities like a husking bee, nutting, clam-digging, and sleigh-riding are described. Finally, Yankee diction is rendered with precision:

"Sam, what are you bothering yourself about Mr. Linden for?"—"How long since you was made a trustee?" said the squire, beginning his sentence with an untranslatable sort of grunt, and ending it in his teacup.

"Give us the sugar-bowl down this way, Cilly," said Joe, "this apple sarce is as sour as sixty."

"I've been your trustee ever since you was up to anything," said his sister. "Come, Sam—don't you begin now. What's made you so crusty?"—"It ain't the worst thing to be crusty," said the squire, while Joe started up and seized the sugar-bowl. "Shows a man's more'n half baked anyhow."[29]

As an attempted portrait of a New England village, *Say and Seal* is among the most interesting novels that the Warners wrote, but that portrait was, of course, only of secondary significance to them. Their primary concern was the religious allegory at the center of the novel, and as the book progresses, increasingly less attention is given to the portrait of the village, and more attention is given to the allegory. By the end of the novel, interest in the details of local color has virtually disappeared.

## VIII  *Reception*

*Say and Seal* was published in 1860—unfortunately, for at that time national attention was focused on issues of far greater consequence than the regional customs and life of rural New England. Not surprisingly, the book sold poorly, but it did receive some good critical attention. In England, it was compared favorably with George Eliot's *Adam Bede* and described as an "extraordinary work" and as "one of Miss Wetherell's most finished and successful efforts."[30] Perhaps the most interesting of the American reviews was

the one that appeared in the *Atlantic Monthly*, then the bastion of
New England literature and thought. The reviewer, F. C. Hopkinson, claimed that "Our real American novels may be counted on our
fingers, while the tales that claim the name may be weighed by the
ton."[31] Among novels that could truly be considered American were
those by Nathaniel Hawthorne, Harriet Beecher Stowe, George
William Curtis—and Susan Warner. "Miss Warner's books," he
said, "have always a genuine flavor of originality, and an acute, living appreciation of Yankee character, that give them a right to rank,
unchallenged, as real and valuable novels. In their simplicity, their
freshness, their quiet humor and not less quiet fun, their frequent
narrowness and stiffness, and their deep and true religious senti-
ment, they have the real essence of the New England character."[32]
"We have never seen," Hopkinson concluded, "the drollery of a
genuine Yankee to more advantage than in 'Say and Seal' "; and he
supported the claim with extensive quotations from the book.[33]

It is interesting that Hopkinson and other reviewers thought that
*Say and Seal* was solely Susan's work rather than a novel written
jointly with her sister. In fact, *Say and Seal* is very unlike most of
Anna's work. Her better known fiction, as we have seen, tends to be
literal, not allegorical; and aside from *Say and Seal*, she wrote little
that suggests that she cared much about the details of New England
life and customs and their potential value for literature. The critics
had reason to consider Susan as the sole author of *Say and Seal*. In
fact, it seems likely that while the book was written jointly, it was
written to her specifications, not Anna's.

CHAPTER 5

# We Would See Jesus

So we worked! Big books, little books; now and then an article for some paper or magazine. We corrected compositions for a certain school; we wrote dictation papers for the teachers. We made our own dresses, and kept the household bills at the most modest figure. But never forgetting what my sister repeats [sic] so often, how good God was to us. What can equal the sweetness of that constant thought? or steady one's heart, like the quiet words, 'Your Father knoweth.'

—Anna Warner, *Susan Warner*[1]

## I   *The Publishers*

Robert Carter was born in Scotland, emigrated to America in 1831, and four years later, established a bookstore on Canal Street in New York City. In 1836, James Lenox, a man of considerable wealth and prestige in the city, recommended that Carter publish a particular religious book on the atonement. Carter agreed to do it, and the book became the first of hundreds of religious books that he published in the years that followed. By the mid-nineteenth century, he was a man of much importance and influence in the evangelical Protestant movement. "He was so careful in regard to publishing nothing that he could not approve," wrote his biographer, "that he seldom published anything he had not read. There were a few of his authors whose opinions he was as sure of as he was of his own, and whose writings he accepted without reading."[2] A member of the Board of Managers of the American Bible Society, a founder of the New York Sabbath Committee, and a member of the Board of Foreign Missions, Carter was the close friend and associate of ministers and missionaries; indeed, his biographer claimed that ". . . there was no layman in this country more largely known among the clergy than Robert Carter."[3]

Carter's friendships had obvious value for the authors whose works he published. After all, if a book were recommended from the pulpit, it was surely on its way to selling well and reaching a large audience. There were decided advantages to being published by Carter—advantages which even the large, well-known commercial firms like Putnam's and Harper and Brothers' could not offer.

Carter's religious commitments and interests made him an ideal and sympathetic publisher for the Warners' books; yet when he was first offered *The Wide, Wide World* for publication, he returned the manuscript unread. He more than compensated for the error, however, for the sisters eventually became two of his most popular and profitable authors. Putnam published most of the Warners' books in the 1850's, but in 1853, Carter issued Susan's *The Law and the Testimony*, a volume of biblical extracts. A decade later, he was the sisters' principal publisher.[4]

The move from Putnam to Carter signalled an increasing didacticism in the Warners' novels—indeed the move made this possible: Putnam was a commercial publisher who sought to please a general audience, but Carter directed his wares solely at religious readers. Of course, the Warners' books had always been didactic; but in their fiction published by Carter, plot and characterization were reduced to the simplest outlines, essentially so that they would not interfere with, or distract from, the didactic message.

## II  *Books for Carter*

Susan Warner wrote two series of novels—known, respectively, as Stories on the Lord's Prayer (also called the Say and Do series) and A Story of Small Beginnings—which are really nothing more than religious and moral lessons strung out along thin narrative lines. The books in these series are of absolutely no literary pretension or literary value. Pine Needles, a volume in the Lords's Prayer series, may be taken as an example of the type.

The novel's plot, what little there is of it, concerns the Candlish sisters, Maggie and Esther, who invite Meredith Franklin and his sister Flora to spend part of the autumn at Mosswood, the Candlish home on the Hudson River. Not long after the Franklins arrive, Fenton Candlish, Maggie and Esther's older brother, and Eban Murray, their uncle, join them. Each day a picnic lunch is packed, and everyone goes outdoors to spend the day. Much of the time is spent listening to Meredith, who reads the others various articles. In turn, the articles prompt questions—particularly from Maggie, the pleasantest and most intelligent of the girls—about a formidable

array of topics extending from Norse mythology to the nature of a
Christian's duty to others. The book has no formal conclusion and
ends abruptly after an account of one of the picnics. There is little
characterization aside from a contrast between Fenton and
Meredith. The former enjoys such "low pleasures" as wine, which,
says Meredith, "brings people into the gutter."[5] On the other hand,
Meredith, who, like the others, is fairly rich, proposes that as a
steward of the Lord's money, he should establish a chapel for poor
Christians who live far from a church.

The "plot" is, of course, only a loose framework within which the
author could give her readers moral and religious instruction, and,
to be sure, moral and religious instruction can be found on virtually
every page.

*Pine Needles* is perhaps more interesting, at least biographically,
than most of the author's other minor didactic fiction because it is
set at Constitution Island. Mosswood is patterned after the
Warners' home, and the various places in which the picnics take
place are recognizably locations on Constitution Island and along
the banks of the river. The settings are, however, described only in
general terms; and the reader who was not acquainted with
Constitution Island or who missed the references to West Point,
Fort Montgomery, and so forth would have little reason to conclude
that the author was using settings that she knew well. It is only a
generalized sense of nature that she gives, with little concrete,
geographic reality. Like the narrative and characterization, the
sense of place in this book and in Susan's other minor didactic fiction is vague and weak.

### III   *"The Word"*

Susan and Anna Warner wrote a series of books, collectively entitled "The Word", in which they gave a chapter-by-chapter, verse-
by-verse interpretation of the Bible. The series was published by
Carter. "We thought," wrote Anna, "that it would be good to go
over the Bible story, for children; not in the least re-writing, adap-
ting, or expurgating, but searching out and setting forth all the light
which manners and customs, geography and travellers explorations,
really threw upon the Bible story."[6]

The sisters read several works on the Bible—the authorities they
consulted, Anna claimed, were only the best—and then set out to
put what they had learned into a form that would be both enter-

taining and instructive for children. It was decided that Susan would deal with the Old Testament, Anna with the New. The former's *Walks from Eden* (1865) dealt primarily with Genesis and was followed by *The Star out of Jacob* (1866), *The House of Israel* (1866), and *The Kingdom of Judah* (1878). The books are structured simply; in *Walks from Eden*, for example, members of a family—several children, their grandmother, and their uncle—leave the city to spend some time in the country. Each day is devoted to general discussion of episodes in the Bible, the geography of biblical stories, and explications of difficult passages. The book has no formal conclusion, nor is there any indication, aside from a brief note in the preface, that a sequel is to follow.

"The aim of this work," according to the preface, "is not commentary nor fiction. It is, in the strictest form, *truth*. The Bible narrative is a skeleton. We wish, by the aid of collateral facts, to clothe the skeleton in its living flesh and blood. Or so to set forth the Bible incidents and course of history, with its train of actors, as to see them in the circumstances and colouring, the light and shade, of their actual existence."[7] She had used, she said, "whatever research and travel have made sure, with recent science and discovery, to fill up what is sketchy and clear up what is not plain; thus entering as far as we may, into the simple truth of the things, the times, the actors."[8]

The sisters had appropriated for themselves a subject—biblical exegesis—which was traditionally reserved for learned theologians. Whatever scholars and theologians may have thought when they found their ideas and discoveries being popularized by the sisters, the public was apparently grateful. The books were favorably commented on, frequently reissued, and kept in print until the early years of the twentieth century. With pardonable pride, Anna wrote that ". . . a gentleman fresh from the Holy Land, said that, next to the Bible, these books of my sister's were his *best* guide-books over there"—praise indeed since neither sister ever crossed the Atlantic.[9] They based their descriptions in The Word solely on their readings.

## IV  *The Perfect Child*

Throughout the 1860's, the Warners provided Carter with books that sold well but that were of little or no literary interest. These books generally received little critical attention, but the heroine of

one of them was attacked in *Blackwood's* as insufficiently virtuous—a charge that must have astounded the Warners.[10] In fact,
the critic found little to support his criticism. The Warners' heroes
and heroines were seldom anything but perfect.

The only Warner novels from the 1860's, aside from *Say and Seal*,
with any significant literary value are *Melbourne House* (1864),
*Daisy* (1868), and *Daisy: Second Series* (1868)—a trilogy concerned
with another of Susan Warner's ideal young girls, Daisy Randolph.
The books are not up to earlier standards, however. Characterization in these novels, particularly *Melbourne House*, is thin, and
Daisy is never as fully characterized as the author's earlier heroines,
Ellen Montgomery and Fleda Ringgan. Daisy's world is as unsympathetic and occasionally as cruel as Ellen's, and she confronts
social and moral difficulties with an assurance and self-reliance that
matches Fleda's; but there are few other similarities. In general,
Daisy exists only as an exemplar of the author's moral principles;
there is little sense, until the final volume in the trilogy, of any psychological reality.

*Melbourne House* is the least ambitious of the three books. Daisy
is introduced as a rich, well-mannered girl, who, much to her
mother's distress, has been taught to read and study her Bible by a
Mr. Dinwiddie. Daisy's mother has little use for religion and wants
her daughter to concern herself with money and social standing and
to be beautiful, submissive, and vain. With some encouragement
from family friends and her father, however, Daisy rejects her
mother's goals and does only what she thinks most Christian. The
conflict between mother and daughter is not resolved in this book.
(Nor, for that matter, is it resolved in the two volumes that follow.
At the end of the last in the series, Daisy and her mother have made
a truce with each other, but neither has materially changed her
position.) *Melbourne House* ends abruptly with her parents' deci-
sion to send Daisy south to a plantation owned by the family.
Daisy's father has been injured in an accident, and a doctor has
recommended that he go to Europe to recuperate. His wife and his
son Ransom have decided to accompany him, but it is thought best
that Daisy remain in this country, away from her mother.

Like many of Susan Warner's novels, *Melbourne House* is
basically a series of loosely related episodes, each of which il-
lustrates a moral principle. In one episode, Daisy teaches a cripple
to have faith in God; in another, she teaches a poor child to read;

and in a third, she convinces her father to give a party for the people who work on his estate. Daisy is an epitome of faith, hope, and charity—not really a person, but an exemplar of virtues.

If *Melbourne House* has any literary interest, beyond serving as an introduction to the two novels that follow it, it is as a forerunner of a hugely popular series of novels for children, the Elsie Dinsmore books by Martha Farquharson Finley. The first of the twenty-eight novels in this series appeared in 1867, three years after *Melbourne House*, and the last in the series was published in 1905. The books reputedly sold millions of copies and made a fortune for their author. Apparently their turgid prose and priggish heroine still have readers, for some of the books are still in print. Elsie Dinsmore bears a clear resemblance to Ellen Montgomery, especially in their shared ability to shed tears at the slightest provocation; but it was Daisy Randolph, not Ellen, who provided Finley with the main outlines of her heroine. Elsie "inherited" Daisy's unblemished character, her Southern plantation, and her indulgent father—but not her uncharitable mother. Like Daisy, Elsie spends her days brooding about religious issues. The best-known episode in the Elsie books occurs in the first volume when Elsie refuses to play a secular tune on the piano on Sunday, for this, she says, would profane the Sabbath. Her father insists that she remain sitting on the piano stool until she has played the song; she stays there—until she passes out. Her father, now somewhat remorseful, sees her point—and promptly becomes a Christian. Virtually the same episode occurs in *Melbourne House*, when Daisy refuses her parents' request to sing an opera tune on Sunday. Her father eventually comes to see her point, although, of course, her mother does not; and so Daisy, who has made a convert of her father, is whipped by her mother for disobedience.

Daisy and Elsie are morally superior to their parents; and if we are to find an explanation for the great attraction that these rather priggish and self-righteous heroines had for young nineteenth-century readers, it is perhaps to be found in this moral superiority. Both heroines make clear that they know the will of God and that they will obey their parents *only* if the parents, too, obey the will of God. Absurd as Daisy and Elsie appear to today's readers, their moral independence—indeed their moral imperiousness—must have been rather sobering to parents and welcome to children living in an age in which it was thought that children should be seen and not heard. In fact, *Melbourne House* and the Elsie books, far from being innocuous or merely silly, were rather insidious. Under the guise of preaching an ideal morality, they taught children, in effect, to disobey their parents—and gave good Christian reasons for doing so. There were, of course, other heroines who proved themselves morally superior to their parents; most famous of all was Little Eva in Harriet Beecher Stowe's *Uncle Tom's Cabin* who, on her deathbed, brought her father to Christ. Seldom, however, was the message announced as clearly as it was in the Elsie books and in *Melbourne House.*

## V   *The South*

*Daisy*, the first sequel to *Melbourne House*, is divided into three narrative sections, the first of which concerns Daisy's life at Magnolia, a family plantation which she will someday inherit. Here she is cared for by her aunt and a governess, Miss Dinshon. Her only companion of her own age is her cousin Preston, who argues with her that there is nothing wrong with the slave system and considers the slaves wholly inferior to their white masters. Daisy, on the other hand, protests against the slave system and says that if she were of age and legally entitled to do so, she would free her slaves—an idea scorned by other whites, who remind her that if she were to free her slaves, she would soon be poor. Daisy also protests against the cruel way the overseer, Mr. Edwards, treats the slaves, but she is basically less interested in their material well-being than in the fact that they have no church or religious life. She organizes prayer meetings for them; and of course, this, too, is scorned by the whites. At last Daisy is sent north to a school for young ladies, a school attended largely by Southerners and Southern sympathizers. Daisy finds no friends there; she is scorned both for her religious ideals and for her Northern sympathies. The account of Daisy's life at the school occupies the central portion of the book, and most of the last portion is concerned with a trip she takes to West Point, where her cousin Preston is a student. Daisy, who is now fifteen or sixteen years old, meets a West Point cadet, Christian Thorwold, who shares most of her religious ideals and Northern sympathies. By the end of the novel, Daisy has fallen in love with him, and he has gone to Washington to join the Union army, while Preston has gone south to join the Confederate forces.

With considerable reason, one reviewer concluded that Daisy was "the most wearisome and self-complacent little bore that . . . Miss

Warner ever invented."[11] If Daisy's moral egotism and sententiousness are objectionable in *Melbourne House*, they are doubly so in the sequel. *Daisy* is narrated by the heroine, and so the reader is confronted with the singularly unpleasant situation of a young girl telling how virtuous and beneficent she has been. It is sufficiently unpleasant to hear of Daisy's high principles in not singing secular tunes on Sunday, but at least it is the author who says so; it is far more repugnant—and at times unintentionally amusing—when Daisy tells her readers how good she was to organize Bible readings for her slaves and to skimp on buying her own clothes so that there would be extra money to purchase clothes for one of the servants.

A central problem in the novel is the Southern setting. Like Mrs. Stowe, Susan Warner had never lived in the South. She had never seen a plantation like the one she described in *Daisy*. Her information, like Mrs. Stowe's, may have been derived, at least in part, from fugitive slave narratives and Abolitionist publications; but while Mrs. Stowe was able to transform these materials into what is admittedly the most powerful literary work of the Abolitionist movement, Susan Warner was able, in effect, to do little more than list or state the usual materials of Abolitionist literature: the cruel overseer, the devoted house-servants, the wives sold away from husbands, the children sold away from parents, the poor living conditions, the whippings, and so forth. One of the slaves who is characterized—most are simply names—is Darius, who is almost certainly based on Mrs. Stowe's Uncle Tom. Susan Warner perhaps realized that it had been a mistake to deal with materials that Mrs. Stowe had used so effectively. Although much is made of Daisy's Southern heritage throughout the last two-thirds of the book and throughout *Daisy: Second Series*, the scene never returns to the South. The author must have realized that it was somewhat late to publish a polemic against slavery: when *Daisy* was published, Appomattox was three years in the past.

## VI   *The War*

In the first two volumes of the Daisy series, especially *Melbourne House*, Susan Warner's preoccupation with ideal types prevents any intricate or subtle dramatic development. The moral opposites represented by Daisy and her mother and by Thorwold and Preston are too schematic and too absolute to permit any dramatic suspense or psychological development. Knowing the author's moral stance, the reader is aware from the beginning of each episode exactly how it will end and knows exactly the moral roles each character will play. The episodes in the first two books in the series are ritualistic, not so much proving the superiority of good over evil as reenacting the triumph of good. In part, *Daisy: Second Series* is like its predecessors: here again, episodes are really miniature, ritualistic examples of the triumph of good. In this novel, however, the author attempted something far more ambitious than she had in the earlier volumes. Here Daisy's successive moral victories are paralleled to the victory in the Civil War of the North over the South. As seen in this novel, the war is, like Daisy's life, a ritual in which God shows that those who follow his laws will ultimately triumph. The novel attempts to show a parallel between one's personal destiny and the larger scheme of history.

In the opening chapters, Daisy goes to Washington where the Northern army is being assembled. Here she sees Thorwold again but is soon called to Europe to join her parents, whom she has not seen for several years. Thorwold as a soldier for Christ goes into battle to free the slaves; Daisy, as the author makes clear, is also a soldier for Christ and has her own war to win—the war against parents who adamantly sympathize with the South and particularly against her mother, who is as opposed to Daisy's moral and religious position as she was before she and her daughter were separated. Appropriately, the chapters concerned with Daisy's life abroad are titled "Skirmishing," "A Victory," "A Truce," "Old Battlefields." Daisy achieves a victory of sorts when she obtains her father's consent to continue her friendship with Thorwold, even though he is a Union soldier. Shortly after this concession, her father dies, and Daisy returns to America with her mother. Her brother, meanwhile, has joined the Confederate troops. Preston is wounded in battle and is in a hospital in Washington. Against the advice of her friends, Daisy goes to Washington to nurse him; and while she is there, Thorwold is brought in, mortally wounded. After his death, she returns to Melbourne House, her Southern properties having been devastated by the war. For the present, she will care for her mother but hopes eventually to return to the South and teach in a Freedman's school.

There is much less moralizing, much less sententious preaching in this novel than in the two that preceded it. Daisy is given ample opportunity to prove her undoubted virtuousness, but much of the book is devoted to descriptions of the war and its progress. The narrative is smoother and has a more interesting design than that of other books in the series. The first book is, after all, merely episodic; there is no real narrative progress but rather a series of episodes exemplifying various ideals. *Daisy*, although a more interesting book than its predecessor, is seriously marred by its choice of narrator and setting. However, *Daisy: Second Series* develops a narrative of considerable dramatic interest by paralleling an individual's life with a large historical event—a narrative device which, incidentally, had earlier been popularized by the novels of Sir Walter Scott and James Fenimore Cooper. In any consideration of the use of the Civil War in fiction, *Daisy: Second Series* deserves attention. Not only is its narrative structure of interest; it also documents the Northerners' attitude toward the war as a holy mission—not simply a political or economic matter, but a God-directed movement to overcome the forces of evil.

All three of the novels received some poor reviews; and in *The Nation*, a review of the final volume concluded that ". . . no one who has followed [Daisy's] progress thus far will be sorry to see her put finally on the shelf."[12] But the public apparently disagreed. The books remained in print for more than fifty years. As late as 1920, a new edition of *Daisy* was published, and the following year, the remaining two volumes were reissued.

### VII   A Whig to the End

In January, 1860, Susan Warner wrote in her journal that she and Anna were "projecting" *Wych Hazel*, but that they were not very enthusiastic about it.[13] Money was needed, however, and the sooner another novel was completed, the sooner they could meet expenses. In early October, she reported that the book was "well under way" and she was clearly optimistic about its future.[14] Three months later, the book was finished, and she was preparing a final draft. But she was dissatisfied with the book; it didn't "seem strong and graphic and nervous"; and in fact, it was set aside.[15] Early in the 1870s, however, the sisters returned to the project. When it was finally published in 1876, it was printed in two volumes, *Wych Hazel* and *The Gold of Chickaree*. Together, they constitute one novel; the division between them is altogether arbitrary.

The *Wych Hazel* books are an ambitious attempt to characterize the full span of American society. The books are not, however, novels of manners but novels of social criticism. Their proposals for improving the lives of laborers—and eliminating the pleasures of wealth—would have seemed revolutionary in America in 1876; and perhaps this, in the nation's centennial year, was exactly the impression that the sisters wanted to give. As novels of social criticism, *Wych Hazel* and *The Gold of Chickaree* are exceedingly ambitious, and their utopian solutions for the social inequities brought about by American capitalism deserve the attention of cultural as well as literary historians.

The *Wych Hazel* books reflect certain biases of evangelical Protestantism and more noticeably the political biases that the sisters had acquired from their father. Indeed, in 1859, the year before they started their books, Henry Whiting Warner had argued in *Fifty Years Progress* that although "Our American institutions are . . . spoken of as democratic . . . they were not such at first; and if they are ever to become such, God help us!"[16] "Assemblies of the multitude," he said, ". . . can never have the requisite knowledge, the requisite sobriety of thought and action, the requisite predominance of public principle and virtue, to manage the affairs of a nation prudently and wisely."[17] He was dismayed by the growing political and social influence of immigrants and warned against "the fearful amount of foreign mixture that has been pouring in among us of late years, and which is still in flood."[18] Such people, he said, "know nothing of our polity; they have no respect for our religion; the evangelical rigor of our morals annoys and displeases them: our whole civilization is to them a darkness, in which they grope impatiently, but do not see." The immigrants "are but clogs upon our institutions."[19] It was necessary to subject the mass of men to the control of an elite, and Warner thought that this elite could be found among the wealthy. In turn, *Wych Hazel* and *The Gold of Chickaree* exhibit a decided distrust of human nature and assert the need for benevolent people of wealth to control society. The novels are clearly outgrowths of Warner's political and social philosophy.

## VIII  *The Narrative*

At the beginning of the first novel, Wych Hazel and her guardian, Mr. Falkirk, are returning to her family home, Chickaree, from which she has been absent for many years. They travel by stagecoach, and one of the other passengers proves to be Dane Rollo, a neighbor at Chickaree. He takes an increasing interest in her affairs, especially after they have arrived at her home. She assumes that he is in love with her but later learns that there are practical reasons for his attention: by the terms of her father's will, Rollo is her joint guardian with Mr. Falkirk. She also discovers that it was her parents' wish that Rollo become her husband. According to the will, if she, before the age of twenty-five, marries without Rollo and Falkirk's consent, her wealth, aside from a small provision, will be given to Rollo. The will is supposed to protect her from fortune hunters, but simultaneously it restricts her liberty, and she finds this nearly intolerable. Rollo tells her that he loves her and will be her guardian in name only unless she chooses, by marrying him, to make him legally the guardian of all her affairs. Eventually she does learn to love him, and they are married.

Rollo purchases some mills at Morton Hollow near Chickaree and tries to improve the workers' lot by increasing their salaries and bettering their living conditions. It is his apparent disinterestedness in this matter that is primarily responsible for Wych Hazel's increased admiration. Inspired by Rollo's ideals, she buys a tract of land important to the water-rights for his mills and thereby prevents its purchase by Rollo's competitor. The competitor's business does poorly, and he finally shuts down his mills, leaving several hundred families without a source of income. Rollo buys the mills, and this makes him sole owner of all the mills in Morton Hollow. Together, he and Wych Hazel set out to create here a utopian village in which all of the laborer's needs—physical, spiritual, and intellectual—will be met. Wych Hazel's friends are scandalized by her behavior; she seems a traitor to her class. The utopian experiment works, however; and Wych Hazel and her husband are morally—and materially—rewarded for their efforts. The mills produce more than they ever have, and the milltown becomes a place of "respectable comfort and real and hopeful life."[20]

Most of the social philosophy that underlies the utopian experiment is Rollo's, though some of the ideas are his wife's. Rollo insists, among other things, that laborers should not work more than twelve hours a day, should be well paid, and should be more than twelve years of age—self-evident principles today but uncommon a century ago. Wych Hazel's assertion that day care be publicly available to working mothers would still seem controversial in some places today. Essentially what Rollo and Wych Hazel want to do is provide middle-class life for laborers. He builds new homes for his workers, gives them a library (with "a reading room for the women and one for the men"), and opens a store with prices "at little over wholesale prices."[21] He builds two churches—"one would not accommodate the population"—and devotes a large portion of the land in Morton Hollow to a park with "groves and lawns, walks and seats under the trees; prepared places for cricket and base ball and gymnastic exercises; swings for the children."[22] The village includes public baths, a bank, schools where designers and mechanics can be educated, and a "home for the disabled and superannuated old people."[23] Morton Hollow looks like a middle-class community—there are even white picket fences around the houses—and provides all the middle-class comforts. Although "his business has grown and spread and increased," Rollo has returned his profits to his workers in the form of social services and higher wages.[24]

The *Wych Hazel* books are rather sweeping or utopian, if not entirely original, in their proposals for social reform—but it is important to note how ineffective such proposals proved to be historically. The social reforms in the Warners' books depend upon the Christian character and ideals of Rollo and his wife—and the fact that they are wealthy. Were they not wealthy or, for that matter, not Christians, their social reforms would never have been realized. The Warners insisted that individuals, not governments, should bring about social improvements. They shared their father's distrust in democracy; they believed, like him, that a patrician group was needed to control society. This group would organize society according to patrician ideals—and this is exactly what happens in the novels. What the Warners failed to realize was the probable dangers involved in consigning economic, political, and social decisions to any elite; surely there are few men as consistently disinterested as Rollo.

## IX  The Perfect Woman

The *Wych Hazel* books trace the moral and social growth of the heroine from a thoughtless and self-centured girl to what the Warners considered an ideal, virtuous woman. At first, the heroine seems independent and emotionally self-sufficient, and she is rich enough to remain single and make her way through life without help from men. By the end of the second book, however, she no longer wants her freedom or her wealth and is content to submit her will to her husband's. At the beginning of *Wych Hazel*, she is light-hearted and indifferent to, or unaware of, moral responsibility. She is described as "the young heiress, the young mistress of fabulous acres"; she is "the new beauty, who bid fair to bewitch all the world with hand and feet and gipsy eyes."[25] She considers life a "fairy tale"; and asked what she plans to do with it, she replies simply, "I think I should like to enjoy it. . . ."[26] Rather than be "nice [and] proper," she would like to be "wild witch hazel in the woods, though it's no sort of use. . . ."[27]

Wych Hazel is reminiscent of Capitola, the willful and self-reliant heroine of Mrs. E. D. E. N. Southworth's *The Hidden Hand*, published in 1858, the year before the Warners' novel was begun. *The Hidden Hand* enjoyed an emormous popularity, sold hundreds of thousands of copies, and was dramatized no less than forty times. But a heroine like Capitola had little appeal for the Warners. Sobriety and high moral seriousness, not light-heartedness and "gipsy eyes," were the characteristics of Warner heroines, and so it was not surprising that they would transform a Capitola-like girl into a sober, moral, and submissive wife. In the Warners' terms, a woman is only happy and admirable when she is serious, responsible, and virtuous. They had little interest in women whose purpose in life was merely "to enjoy it." But by the time the *Wych Hazel* volumes were published, however, the public was admiring heroines like Capitola, not those like Wych Hazel, and the moral progress that the Warners traced in their heroine already seemed old-fashioned and misguided.

## X    *The Critics*

In general, the critics attacked the *Wych Hazel* books. They were favorably reviewed in *The Library Table* ("prettily told, this little story, and the publishers have given it a charming dress"), [28] but *Appleton's Journal* said it was "beneath serious criticism."[29]

If "Wych Hazel had been published anonymously, we should have guessed it to be the first production of a "bright" young miss, fresh from school, whose ideas of life were—those of a schoolgirl; whose knowledge of human nature was derived from G. P. R. James's and Bulwer's earlier novels; whose pictures of society were colored by her first ball; and whose conception of religion was developed from penny tracts. And even then we cannot say that we should have regarded it as a remarkably promising production.[30]

The *Atlantic Monthly* thought that the story was "one of no marked merit or originality."[31] *The Gold of Chickaree* was dismissed by the same journal as "a poor story."[32] In a review of the second volume, the critic for *The Nation* claimed that "It would be a bold statement that 'Wych Hazel' needed any continuation, but if it did, nothing more like it could have been produced than the present story."[33]

Certainly the *Wych Hazel* books were published at the wrong time. The Warners' heroine could only have seemed dated, the vestige of an earlier generation; and their social perspective could find few sympathizers in an age that glorified individualism and the accumulation of vast personal fortunes. In 1850, Susan Warner's ideals were shared by the era; she spoke for her age. Yet a quarter-century later, she had lost much of her audience. She and her sister were as far outside the main current of American life and thought as, once, they were within it.

CHAPTER 6

# Final Works

. . . if you enter upon the service of the Lord Jesus, you must remember that you are not your own. You must live to do his service and accept his will, whatever it may cost; and there must be no half-way work. It is a continual service, hour by hour and minute by minute; it means, not living to one's self, and being separate from the world; it means, loving him best.

—Susan Warner, *Daisy Plains*[1]

## I  *Exemplary Behavior*

Between 1877 and her death eight years later, Susan Warner devoted most of her literary efforts to a series of didactic novels much like those that she had earlier written for Carter. Those earlier novels were grouped into series of books related by shared settings and characters. The series of didactic novels that she wrote during the last years of her life, however, were linked to each other only by a shared foundation in historical or biographical fact. All of these novels were introduced by a note stating substantially the same as that which introduced *My Desire:*

Some readers will perhaps be more interested in the following story if they know that it is true. All the great points of the history, the whole framework of facts, are life-work and not fancy. Life-work, lived through so long ago that there is nobody now to be hurt by the telling.[2]

Although she insisted that she was recording fact, all of the later novels are in effect nothing more than extended tracts. The plots of all the novels are simple and unadorned; the author was far less interested in her characters or her story than in the lessons she had to impart. When they were first published, these novels neither received nor in fact deserved serious literary attention. Like other didactic fiction written by Susan and published by Carter, they are decidedly minor works and can be dealt with summarily.

## II  *Submission and Duty*

The first of the series to be published was *Diana* (1877). The heroine Diana Starling and her mother have moved to Pleasant Valley, a village "somewhere in the wilds of New England."[3] Here she meets and falls in love with Lieutenant Evan Knowlton, who is later assigned to a troop on the Western frontier, but who leaves with the "understanding" that he and Diana will marry when he returns. Mrs. Starling, however, does not like Knowlton and intercepts his letters to Diana and burns them. Believing that Knowlton has forgotten her, Daisy marries the local minister, Basil Masters.

From a postmistress, Diana learns that Knowlton had indeed written to her and that the letters were delivered to her mother. Knowlton finally returns to Pleasant Valley and begs her to divorce Masters; but Diana refuses, saying that her duty now lies with the minister. By the end of the book, she is reconciled to her marriage, and she and Masters have determined to move to a factory town near Boston where, they believe, they can be of moral and spiritual help to the people. At the beginning of the book, Diana is willful and light-hearted; by the end, she is resigned to her duty, to fulfilling her marriage vows and devoting her life to the good of others.

Like *Say and Seal*, *Diana* is in part an allegory of the Christian's progress toward salvation. As noted earlier (p. 84), the parallel between, on the one hand, Christ and his church and, on the other, the husband and his wife is frequently mentioned in the Bible. As the church submits itself to Christ, so does the wife submit herself to her husband. The allegorical purpose in *Diana* is obvious: the Christian (Diana) learns to reject the world (Knowlton, the soldier) for Christ (Masters, the minister). Significantly, Diana finds no ultimate meaning or object in life until she learns to submit herself fully to her husband.

The plot of *My Desire* (1879) is similar to *Diana*'s. The heroine, Desire Burgoyne, lives in a rural New England hilltown (Chesterfield, Massachusetts) with her sister Olive and her grandmother. Another sister, Caroline, who lives in Philadelphia, invites Desire to her house for a visit. In Philadelphia, Desire meets and falls in love with a wealthy man named Maxmilian Iredell. After her return to Chesterfield, her sister Olive is invited to Caroline's for a visit, and she in turn meets Iredell and falls in love with him. He is, however, more interested in Desire than Olive; and so, back in the New

England hilltown, when a letter is received announcing his intention to visit the town, Olive contrives to have Desire sent away for an extended visit to friends. Olive now has Iredell to herself and convinces him that she is devoted to him. He proposes to her, and they are married. Many years later, on her deathbed, she confesses to both Iredell and Desire. After Olive's death, Iredell and Desire restate their love for each other and are married.

Desire Burgoyne, like Diana Starling, is essentially a selfless, generous Christian who ultimately finds in religion greater rewards than she would find in worldly goods. Olive marries Iredell for his wealth, but it is the ideal qualities in his character that attract Desire. The novel is intensely moralistic, and most of it is spent contrasting the characters of the two sisters.

*The End of a Coil* (1880) is a long discursive novel concerning a young girl's life at school in Philadelphia and later with her parents in England and Europe. The novel ends with the marriage of the heroine, Dolly Copley, to a man she encountered many years earlier in Philadelphia. Dolly is the usual Warner heroine: socially accomplished, well read, and intensely devout; but there is little incident in her life or, for that matter, in the book's 718 pages. Much of the novel is set in Europe—but the author's observations on life in Europe are exceedingly superficial—as one would expect from an author who had never been east of Boston.

In *The Letter of Credit* (1881), Rotha Carpenter, a young girl, comes with her mother to New York, where they take rooms in a poor section of town. There they are befriended by a man, Digby Southwode, whose father Mrs. Carpenter once nursed back to health. Rotha's mother dies, and she is cared for first by Digby and later by her aunt, Mrs. Serena Busby, a wealthy and influential woman who hopes to marry her daughter to Digby. He, however, is clearly interested in Rotha, and so Mrs. Busby tries to keep them apart. Her attempts fail, however, and Rotha and Digby are married. Much of the novel is spent describing Rotha's moral and spiritual education and contrasting her disinterested motivations with her aunt's selfish behavior.

## III  *Further Perfection*

The next "factual" novel to be published was *Nobody* (1882). Lois Lothrop, the heroine, visits her aunt in New York and meets Philip Dillwyn, a young man of good family. She returns to her home in rural New England where she lives with her grandmother and her sisters. Dillwyn arranges for a woman to live with and tutor the Lothrop girls. After the grandmother's death, Lois takes a job as a teacher. Meanwhile, as becomes a typical Warner heroine, she has converted Dillwyn to Christianity, and in the final pages of the book, they are married.

Lois is as moralistic and pietistic as her predecessors among Susan Warner's heroines; indeed, she tells Dillwyn that she could never marry him if he were not a devout Christian. Curiously, at the time she says this, he has already been converted to Christianity—yet she is not aware of what would, presumably, be a marked change in his character. "It is amazing," one reader pointedly remarked,

that Miss Warner does not see how she has stultified herself by her representation that this change is a matter of such vital consequence that the girl will break her heart rather than marry the man without it, and yet it is so little a thing that in all the weeks since his return she has never suspected anything of it. Her surprise at his announcement is proof of that. The answer to such a criticism would be, that she *would* have felt the difference, and that therein is Miss Warner's mistake. Either way, it is an instance of the unreality which makes most of the "religious novels" positively dangerous. One kind of mind they disaffect, another they mislead, while it is not easy for a critic to deal with them, from the difficulty of separating their false views of the truth from the truth itself, so that the condemnation of the one shall not seem irreverence to the other.[4]

Stephen Kay, the hero of *Stephen, M.D.* (1883), is an orphan who discovers that his mother has left a large unpaid debt, and he goes to work to pay it off. He succeeds and in the process gains the admiration of many. He is "bright, honest, frank, diligent, sober."[5] His rise in the world is rapid. He goes to Harvard, becomes a doctor—acquiring many admirers along the way—and eventually becomes governor of Massachusetts. *Stephen, M.D.* is unusual among the Warner novels in that it is centered on a hero rather than a heroine. The didactic purpose is, however, unchanged; Stephen is a physician of the soul as well as of the body; and he effects as many religious conversions as physical cures.

In *A Red Wallflower* (1884), the heroine Esther Gainsborough is in love with Pitt Dallas, but their families have various religious disagreements with each other, and his family actively prevents him from seeing her or—after she has moved away—knowing her whereabouts. He eventually locates her, however; the religious differences are resolved; and they are married.

Except for the opening chapters—which concern a runaway slave—most of *Daisy Plains* (1885), named for the New England village in which much of the action is set, concerns the childhood, youth, and marriage of Helen Thayer, another of Susan Warner's pious and moral heroines. For various reasons, she is married to the wrong man, a Professor L'Estrange, rather than to Mr. Somers, whom she loves. But in the end, she and Somers, like Diana Starling in *Diana*, are resigned to the situation; they know that "they had missed their ideal" but know "also that the real which they had in hand was to be used and invested for the Lord's glory. . . ."[6]

*Daisy Plains* was, incidentally, left nearly complete at the author's death and the final touches were her sister's. In *Patience* (1890) and *West Point Colors* (1903), Anna also wrote extended didactic tales based on fact. Susan Warner's "factual" novels were at least modestly popular, but Anna's seem to have passed virtually unnoticed. *West Point Colors*, almost alone among novels by the sisters, was never reprinted in this country.

The prodigious length of the "factual" novels—they average between six and seven hundred pages in length—is largely due to extensive moral dialogues, of which the following, from *The Letter of Credit*, is a representative example. The speakers are Rotha Carpenter and her mother.

"I would like to be a Christian, mother, if it would make you feel easy; but—somehow—I don't want to."

"I know that."

"How do you know that?"

"Because you hold off. If you were once willing, the thing would be done."

There was silence again; till Rotha suddenly broke it by asking,

"Mother, can I help my will?"

"What do you mean?"

"Why! If I don't want to be a Christian, can I make myself want to?"

"That seems to me a foolish question," said her mother. "Suppose you do not want to do something I tell you to do; need that hinder your obeying?"

"But this is different."

"What is being a Christian, then?"

"You know, Rotha."

"But tell me, mother. I don't know if I know."

"You ought to know. A Christian is one who loves and serves the Lord Jesus."

"And then he can't do what he has a mind to," said Rotha.
"Yes, he can; unless it is something wrong."
"Well, he can't do *what he has a mind to*; he must always be asking."
"That is not hard, if one loves the Lord."

This is only a brief portion of the dialogue; and the subject—how does one become a Christian—is one that Rotha discusses frequently throughout the novel. Similar discussions can be found in all the other "factual" novels (and most of Susan's other fiction). The lesson in each of these discussions is essentially the same: "A Christian is one who loves and serves the Lord Jesus." It is in turn the lesson that all of Susan and Anna's fiction teaches; but while their early didactic novels, particularly Susan's, surrounded that lesson with rich narrative materials, in the later novels it formed merely the center of long repetitive discussions. The discussions—all of them as impersonal and stylized as the one quoted above—dilute and weaken narratives that are already too simple to sustain six or seven hundred pages of fiction.

## IV  *Final Years*

During the thirty years between 1885, when her sister died, and 1915, Anna published relatively little. Her biographies of her sister, George Ainslie, and James Stokes and Caroline Phelps Stokes, date from these years. The Stokes biography deserves more attention than historians have given it, but there is nothing in these biographies—or in the tracts and didactic fiction published in these same years—to interest the literary critic. Susan Warner's novels remained popular, but it was clear that Anna would be remembered, if at all, for *Dollars and Cents* and for her collaborative efforts with her sister, particularly *Say and Seal*. In the years immediately following Anna's death in 1915, however, even that slight residue of her once widespread fame began to vanish.

By the 1930's, even *Queechy* and *The Wide, Wide World* had lost both their critical and their popular following. If critics mentioned them at all, it was to ridicule the emotional excesses of religious and sentimental fiction, and this was exactly the critical treatment one would have expected. The social, political, and religious worlds for which these novels had been written were long dead; without an historical understanding of life in mid-nineteenth-century America, the critic could not be expected to read them sympathetically or to understand their once enormous popularity.

In 1936, the New York State Educational Department proposed honoring the sisters by erecting a bronze marker near the Jason Warner house in Canaan. The marker was made but not erected. For reasons unknown, it was stored at a public garage where it was neglected and forgotten. It was discovered there a decade later and was finally erected beside the road in front of the Warner house. "Many of the scenes in the *Wide Wide World*, and *Queechy*, it reads "were laid in and around this house where Susan and Anna Warner, noted American Authors, spent several summers." The marker may have satisfied local pride, but it must have confused more than one passing motorist, as ignorant of the Warners' names as of their once-popular fiction.

For many years, the Warners and their books were memorialized in the yearly meetings of a rather prestigious organization known as the Martelaer's Rock Association. (Martelaer's Rock was an early name for Constitution Island.) The association included in its membership a number of socially august names not usually connected with literary endeavors—Harriman, Fish, Livingston, Roosevelt, Van Cortlandt, and many others. Among the organization's patrons was J. P. Morgan. One wonders, with reason, why so many bluebloods flocked to honor the sisters at a time when libraries were disposing of long-unread copies of *Queechy* and *The Wide, Wide World*. Perhaps it was because portions of the sisters' rather conservative social and political values were shared by those very rich individuals and families who joined the organization. In any case, it was the sort of social attention that the Warners, remembering their days on St. Mark's Place, would certainly have appreciated. For writers who found moral and social excellence in a patrician class, this was posthumous fame of a most welcome kind.

CHAPTER 7

# A Place in History

NEWS today of the engagement of ————— and —————. The nicest engagement I ever heard of. Well—there came a vision of the great gladness upon some eyes just now—a vision that has merely looked in at our windows and passed by! And then I thought, afterwards, I was rather glad there was nothing between Christ and me.
                                        —Susan Warner, journal entry, September [?], 1873[1]

## I  *Evangelical America*

One of the anecdotes about her forebears that Anna enjoyed telling concerned a merchant, a distant ancestor who sailed with his ship and cargo to Constantinople, where he became fatally ill. Moslems there told him that if he converted to Islam, his ship and cargo would be returned home after his death, and he would be buried in the earth—but if he failed to convert, "ship and cargo [would] be confiscated, and [he would] be put in the sand below high-water mark."[2] But the merchant replied that his family could survive without his wealth, and he was unconcerned with what happened to his body, but he valued his soul too much to lose it. He remained a Christian at his death; the ship and cargo were confiscated, and ". . . his grave was dug in the sea-swept sand, somewhere along the Turkish coast."[3]

The man who placed the highest value not on his wealth or his family but on his Christian soul (his Protestant soul, of course) assumed heroic and ideal proportions to a substantial number of the Warners' contemporary Americans. Already there were those who questioned the supremacy of Protestant theology in American life (Andrew Jackson, as we have seen, was among them) and there were also many who were far more interested in piling up their riches on earth rather than heaven. Large Catholic migrations to America had begun, although, in fact, the new arrivals had as yet had little effect on the mainstream of American religious thought. An occasional observer like Henry Whiting Warner was entirely aware of the effect that the arrivals would have on American life and particularly on its religious thought; yet, at least for the moment, evangelical Protestantism dominated the nation's moral and religious life.[4] Perhaps for the last moment in American history it was possible to say that Protestant theology was at the very center of American life—as it had been for more than two hundred years.

The religious bias expressed in the Warners' novels reflected a national disposition. Their evangelical Protestant persuasion was shared nationally, and to understand the enormous popularity of these novels, one must begin with their religious nature and the fact that, as we have seen, they did not emphasize the teachings of any one Protestant sect. The Warners' fiction appealed to all sects that subscribed to the ideals of evangelical Protestantism. These included the great majority of Protestant American sects and, therefore, the great majority of Americans.

Evangelicalism in America was at its peak of popular acceptance in the 1850s when the Warners' best-known novels were published; and although it has never disappeared as a religious force in this country and, from time to time, has strongly reasserted itself, its national influence declined in the post-Civil War years. Not surprisingly, the Warners' novels, like the religious principles that they preached, were far more warmly received in the 1850s and the 1860s than they were ever received again. Surely if ever there was a novel that was explicitly the statement of a particular historical moment, it was *The Wide, Wide World*.

## II  *The American Novel*

Caroline Kirkland, a well-known novelist, editor, and critic, reviewed *The Wide, Wide World*, *Queechy*, and *Dollars and Cents* for the *North American Review* in 1853. Her extensive review—nearly eight thousand words long—considered the novels as expressions of the national character. Although *Dollars and Cents* seemed to Mrs. Kirkland comparatively "modest" and "less potent" than the other two books, she believed that all three were major literary works, and that their "spontaneous popularity" offered "an index of the national character."[5] If one understood these books, she suggested, one would understand the age and the country that produced them.

She opened her review by asking why the novels of Ann Radcliffe and Charlotte Smith no longer had a popular following. The modern imagination, it seemed, was more concerned with the workings of the factory system than with the "thrilling adventures, delicate shades of character, and love deferred by incredibly fiendish machinations" to be found in earlier fiction.[6] In fact, the sentimentality and high melodrama of Radcliffe's novels could be found in much contemporary fiction, including the Warners' novels; yet it is true that sentimentality and melodrama were now tempered by a concern for realism. The popular American novels of the 1850s were a curious blend of realism and the fantasies of the earlier sentimental novels. Thwarted love mingled as narrative material with a concern for social reform. *Uncle Tom's Cabin* is the most famous example of the type: a book that tried to entertain its readers while it simultaneously tried to reform them.

Mrs. Kirkland believed that American novelists like Catharine Maria Sedgwick and James Fenimore Cooper had been interested in realistic details of American life merely because of their quaint or picturesque nature. Better novelists than they, she believed, would deal with American materials with greater understanding—and this, she contended, was exactly what the Warners were doing. Their novels were important first as realistic statements of American life.

Furthermore, as she saw it, the Warners possessed a moral sensibility that was essential to great fiction but that was lacking in earlier American novels. "To teach morals has been no very direct aim of our indigenous novels. They have breathed a high and pure tone, but it has been an undertone."[7] Susan Warner, she felt, gave religion in her novels "no higher than its due place, and [ascribed] to it no wider than its real influence."[8] Moral and religious earnestness combined with a fine sense of realistic detail; the ideal mingled with the real; and the result was fiction of the first rank. On the one hand, the Warner books were "no whit too religious;" and on the other, "their graphic truth"—specifically "their pictures of American country life and character"—was nowhere equalled.[9]

*The Wide, Wide World, Queechy,* and *Dollars and Cents* belonged to no established type of fiction—rather, said Mrs. Kirkland, they created their own: "humane, religious, *piquant,* natural, national."[10] The Warners appealed "to universal human sympathy" but painted "human nature in its American type."[11] Correspondingly, when a story of real life—American rural life, of the homeliest—unheralded at home, unstamped by foreign approval—lacking the tempting bait of national flattery—and wholly deficient in the flash and flippancy that might attract the vulgar mind, springs at once to a currency which few books ever reach—cried to the skies by the 'most sweet voices,' of old and young, gentle and simple,—we cannot help feeling the verdict to be significant.[12]

Indeed it was a significant verdict, one that American writers were quick to recognize. For more than half a century, local color and religion (or at least a strong moral sensibility) were to inform, often dominate, popular American fiction. *The Wide, Wide World* and other Warner novels have an historical significance that even the casual student of American literature must recognize. These books stand at the very head of the tradition of sentimental, religious best sellers which found their greatest critical and popular approval during the same years that Whitman and Melville were dismissed or overlooked. *The Wide, Wide World* sold hundreds of thousands of copies at a time when Melville's *Pierre* (which criticized the values that the former preached) sold less than three hundred copies. In the simplest terms, the Warners gave American readers what they wanted; Melville antagonized them.

### III   *Ideal and Real*

The early Warner novels—and occasionally the later ones as well—were minutely faithful to the details of American customs and manners; and, therefore, in a sense, these novels can be called realistic. Nonetheless, the sisters' main purpose in writing them was to illustrate ideal moral and religious principles. To illustrate simultaneously ideal principles and real customs was a large order and one which, as we have seen, the Warners were seldom able to fill. To solve the problem, they generally borrowed the duality of late eighteenth- and early nineteenth-century novels by such writers as Maria Edgeworth and Catharine Maria Sedgwick—novels, that is, in which major figures were used to illustrate ideals, while minor figures were characterized by their manners and dialect. This method allowed the novelist to compare ideal standards with ordinary manners and customs—and leave no question as to where the author's preference lay. The incivility that Susan believed was characteristic of rural manners is apparent in the implied contrast of

Aunt Fortune's "bee" and the Marshman's Christmas festivities in *The Wide, Wide World*. Similarly, Fleda in *Queechy* is careful, when discussing others, never to say anything that might be misconstrued and hurt another's feelings; but the local Yankees are rude and openly hostile in their gossip and speculations about others. Such contrasts as these enrich the novels in which they are found, but too often there is no apparent reason for the alternation between realistic descriptions of manners and illustration of ideal principles. It is as if the author were writing two novels at the same time. In *Say and Seal*, for example, there are long descriptions of local customs, and these customs are of considerable interest in themselves—but they have no relation to the book's main objective, which is to outline various ideal principles. The Warners' contemporaries praised them for attending to both American customs and ideals, but this bifocal approach created major, often unresolved, problems in the novels.

## IV  *The Writer and His Age*

The earliest and most popular of the Warners' novels were published in a time of economic, social, and political uncertainties—uncertainties which, in fact, even a civil war did not resolve. The Warners' novels must have been especially welcome because of their emphasis on religion and domesticity—two institutions that even the economic, social, and political problems of the time could not destroy. Susan and Anna's conservative political and social theories, acquired from their father, may have been similarly welcome. Like their father, the sisters valued, as Americans, the concept of liberty, but they were assuredly not libertarians. They considered manners and morals immutable and, therefore, ranked people according to behavior, which they interpreted as the outward sign of moral character.

The Warners' attitude toward women was equally conservative and, therefore, reassuring to those readers (most of them were women) who preferred social and domestic stability to the uncertainties of change. The Warners preached submission to higher authority, the authority of a husband who was himself guided by the immutable standards of manners and morals. However, the woman had "a blessed advantage in the quiet of her sphere; man is tossed by a thousand conflicting cares and interests. But however

with him the needle may fluctuate and vary amid the adverse con-
tacts of the world, let him be sure to find his magnet at home in the
very eye of honor!"[13]

According to the litany, the home, as much as the church, was a
sanctuary of God, and in the home, the mother and wife was the
moral center. Technically, the wife was submissive to her husband's
will; yet in turn, he was submissive to a higher, divine will—and it
was a will which she, as well as he, could decipher. The world outside might be characterized by economic, social, and political
change, but the home remained morally stable and as unchanging
as the divine and immutable laws it obeyed.

In the 1880s, Thomas Wentworth Higginson noted that although
". . . the contributions of American women to the poetry and fiction of the day are abundant and creditable," much of their work
was rapidly forgotten.[14] "Is it so certain," he asked, "that the
women now popular as poets and novelists are securer in their
positions than their predecessors?"[15] In fact, as the attentive student
of American literature knows, much nineteenth-century American
literature by women writers—Alice Brown, Sarah Orne Jewett, and
Catharine Maria Sedgwick, to name some of the best—has been un-
deservedly neglected in this century.[16] Most of this literature is, of
course, didactic and, like the Warners' novels, inextricably tied to
the concerns of its age. The unjust ridicule that until recently was
directed at nineteenth-century domestic novelists like the Warners
is best forgotten. It demonstrates an historical and cultural
naiveté—an ignorance of the cultural environment in which their
domestic novels were written and of the cultural expectations that
these novels fulfilled. Clearly no adequate understanding of
nineteenth-century American literature is possible until the critic
comes to terms with these novels—not according to his own
assumptions and standards (however valid they in another context
might be), but according to theirs.

The Warners wrote primarily to instruct, not entertain; and the
objectives of their fiction were didactic, not aesthetic. The sisters
were far more interested in religion than in literature—and yet
there are portions of *The Wide, Wide World*, *Queechy*, and *Say
and Seal*, among others, that have decided literary as well as
historical value. From time to time, the sisters wrote very well indeed.

The Warners would undoubtedly have been uncomfortable in

literary company—which, in fact, they assiduously avoided. Nonetheless, they deserve a place among the better writers of the age—not, of course, among the more exalted or respected, but at least among such figures as, say, John Greenleaf Whittier, Harriet Beecher Stowe, and other nineteenth-century writers who, while not of the first rank, were integral to the development of American literature.

# Notes and References

## Chapter One

1. Anna Warner, *Susan Warner ("Elizabeth Wetherell")* (New York, 1909), p. 333.

2. Henry James, "The Schönberg-Cotta Family," *The Nation*, I (September 14, 1865), 345.

3. Hudson Square was so prominently a blueblood address that writers frequently used it as the address of upper-class figures in novels. The Effinghams in James Fenimore Cooper's *Home as Found* (1838) live here; and Hudson Square—or St. John's Park as it is called here—also appears in Herman Melville's *Redburn* (1849). Hudson Square was later the site of a freight depot for the Hudson River Railroad. On the site today is the exit pattern of the Hudson Tunnel. Two of the old townhouses, much altered, remain; but nothing remains of the elegance that Henry Whiting Warner found here.

4. Broome Street has changed vastly in the years since the Warners lived here. No. 461 Broome—just to the west of Broadway, once the most fashionable shopping area in the city—was then an entirely respectable address. Before the end of the nineteenth century Broadway was lined by commercial buildings, and much of Broome Street was lined by tenements, warehouses, and factories. The townhouse at 461 was demolished many years ago. The site of the Warners' home in Brooklyn has fared no better: there is nothing left to indicate the site of their farm, the pond nearby, or even the road on which they lived. The hills near their home have been levelled. There is *nothing* to indicate the area which they knew and which Anna described in *Mr. Rutherford's Children*.

5. St. Mark's Place has fared somewhat better than Broome Street and the site of the Warners' home in Brooklyn. Both St. Mark's Place and the surrounding area have suffered from general urban decay, but the Daniel Le Roy house at 20 St. Mark's Place survives to indicate the sort of mansions that once lined the street. Both the Warners' home and the mansion, two doors west, of James Fenimore Cooper were demolished long ago.

6. On Constitution Island was a cottage which the Warners extensively enlarged. In modern perspective, the house is impressively spacious, though architecturally undistinguished. The Warners thought of it as a house for "poor people," and so it must have seemed to their friends who, by and large, were financially well-off and owned substantial country homes. One winter day shortly after *The Wide, Wide World* was published, Susan went outside "and viewed, with odd moralising reflections, the

117

strange old house where we live. How exactly like us—Anna was saying—exactly like a house where poor people live. From that point of view especially,—the discoloured stone end of the house, and bare front walk, looking as if it was not troubled with attentions, and with a kind of uncompromising, cut-loose from-the-world [sic] air—it is just like us. Not ragged yet, not out of repair, though in want of paint. . . ." (*Susan Warner*, pp. 337 - 38)

7. The house is today maintained and opened to the public by the Constitution Island Association. The grounds and gardens near the house look much as they did a century ago, and many of the furnishings inside originally belonged to the family.

8. *Susan Warner*, pp. 200 - 201.

9. Ibid., p. 202.

10. Ibid., pp. 204 - 205.

11. Henry Whiting Warner, *The Liberties of America* (New York, 1853), p. v.

12. Ibid., p. 234.

13. Warner was reared along the strict Calvinist lines of "Old School" Presbyterianism. In Brooklyn, he joined the First Presbyterian Church and transferred his membership to the Mercer Street Church in 1836.

14. Henry Whiting Warner, *An Inquiry into the Moral and Religious Character of the American Government* (New York, 1838), p. 172.

15. George L. Prentiss, *A Discourse in Memory of Thomas Harvey Skinner* (New York, 1871), pp. 58-59.

16. Thomas Harvey Skinner and Edward Beecher, *Hints, Designed to Aid Christians in Their Efforts to Convert to God* (Philadelphia, 1832), p. 42.

17. Ibid., p. 42.

18. Thomas Harvey Skinner, *Religion of the Bible, in Select Discourses* (New York, 1838), pp. 14 - 15.

19. Ibid., p. 323.

20. Skinner and Beecher, *Hints*, pp. 62-64.

21. *Susan Warner*, p. 218.

22. Ibid., p. 236.

23. I have written about the nineteenth-century's idealization of domesticity in *The Civilized Wilderness: Backgrounds to American Romantic Literature, 1817 - 1860* (New York, 1975). See especially chapter five, pp. 132 - 44.

24. The most famous poem idealizing domesticity was John Howard Payne's "Home, Sweet Home." Payne was among Henry Whiting Warner's acquaintances—they were classmates at Union College. I don't know if Payne was also acquainted with Susan, but it would have been an appropriate coincidence if the best-known poet of domesticity were the friend or acquaintance of the best-known novelist of domesticity.

25. Anonymous, "The Birthplace of Washington," *The Gem of the Season for 1849* (New York, n.d.), p. 62.

26. See Barbara Cross, *Horace Bushnell: Minister to a Changing America* (Chicago, 1958) and Katherine Kish Sklar, *Catharine Beecher: A Study in American Domesticity* (New York, 1973). Both of these provide good introductions to the ideals of nineteenth-century domesticity.

27. James, "Schönberg-Cotta," p. 345.

28. Olivia Egleston Phelps Stokes, *Letters and Memories of Susan and Anna Bartlett Warner* (New York, 1925), p. 14.

### Chapter Two

1. Anna Warner, *Susan Warner ("Elizabeth Wetherell")* (New York, 1909), p. 264.

2. Ibid., p. 263

3. Ibid., p. 283

4. Ibid., pp. 344 - 45. The first of these comments is quoted from the *Edinburgh Witness*, the second from the *Newark Daily Advertiser*. The *New York Times* is quoted as saying that ". . . one book like this is not produced in an age."

5. Susan Warner, *The Wide, Wide World* (New York, 1850), I, 84 - 85.

6. Philip Ariès, *Centuries of Childhood: A Social History of Family Life* (New York, 1962). The literature on the history of the family is huge; among the best recent books on the subject is Edward Shorter's *The Making of the Modern Family* (New York, 1975).

7. *Ephesians* V: 22.

8. *The Wide, Wide World*, II, 102.

9. Ibid., I, 340.

10. *Susan Warner*, p. iii.

11. Ibid., pp. 124 - 25.

12. Ibid., p. 166.

13. Ibid., p. 166.

14. Ibid., p. 423.

15. Ibid., p. 177.

16. The Wide, Wide World, I, 308.

17. Ibid., I, 133, 153, 198, 302; II, 83.

18. Ibid., I, 229, 304; II, 118.

19. Ibid., I, 308, 221; II, 82.

20. Ibid., II, 82.

21 Ibid., II, 115, 117.

22. Ibid., II, 47, 63.

23. Caroline Kirkland, review of *The Wide, Wide World, Queechy*, and *Dollars and Cents; The North American Review*, LXXVI (January, 1853), pp. 120 - 21.

24. *The Wide, Wide World*, II, 219.

25. Ibid., II, 72.
26. Ibid., I, 333.
27. Ibid., I, 247.
28. Ibid., I, 167.
29. Ibid., I, 121, 116.
30. Ibid., I, 135.
31. Susan and Anna numbered various Livingstons among their childhood friends; and, even after the sisters were living in virtual poverty, they maintained an acquaintance with Mrs. David Codwise—a Livingston by birth. They were also friendly with Miss Mary Garretson, daughter of Catharine Livingston and niece of Chancellor Robert Livingston. Catharine married the Reverend Freeborn Garretson, a noted Methodist preacher. On Livingston land in Dutchess County, they built a modest but substantial house and surrounded it with a magnificent estate known as Wildercliff. The Warners visited there extensively; and in all probability, it was while visiting there and at other estates nearby that they got background details for *Wych Hazel* and *The Gold of Chickaree*. This was, in any case, good literary country. Not far from Wildercliff was an estate where Henry James as a boy spent much time with relatives, and just down the hill from Wildercliff was a large Gothic mansion at which Edith Wharton spent a portion of her childhood.
32. *The Wide, Wide World*, I, 342.
33. Ibid., I, 343.
34. Anonymous, review of *The Wide, Wide World*, VII (December 28, 1850), 525.
35. John S. Hart, *Female Prose Writers of America* (Philadelphia, 1852), p. 387.
36. Anonymous, review of *The Wide, Wide World*, *Holden's Dollar Magazine*, VII (March, 1851), 136 - 37.
37. Anonymous, review of *The Hills of the Shatemuc*, *Putnam's Monthly*, VIII (November, 1856), 539.
38. Henry James, "The Schönberg-Cotta Family," *The Nation*, I (September 14, 1865), 345.
39. Frank Denham, "How to Drive the Sheriff from the Homestead Door," *New York Times Book Review* (December 24, 1944), p. 8.
40. Henry Nash Smith, "The Scribbling Women and the Cosmic Success Story," *Critical Inquiry*, I (September, 1974), 66.
41. Marion Lochhead, "Stars and Striplings: American Youth in the Nineteenth Century," *Quarterly Review*, V (April, 1959), 184.
42. Van Wyck Brooks, *The Flowering of New England* (New York, 1936), p. 427.
43. Frank Luther Mott, *Golden Multitudes* (New York, 1947), pp. 122, 123.
44. Charles Kingsley, *The Water-Babies* (London, 1903), p. 174.
45. Mott, *Golden Multitudes*, p. 124.

46. Arthur Penn [Brander Matthews], *The Home Library* (New York, 1883), p. 45.

47. Grace Overmyer, "Hudson River Bluestockings—the Warner Sisters of Constitution Island," *New York History*, XL (April, 1959), 137.

48. F. S. D. [sic], "Tears, Idle Tears," *The Critic*, XXI (October 29, 1892), 236.

49. Anonymous, untitled note, *The Illustrated London News*, XCIX (September 12, 1891), 342.

50. Edward G. Salmon, "What Girls Read," *The Nineteenth Century*, XX (October, 1886), 524.

51. Anonymous, review of *Wych Hazel*, *The Nation*, XXII (June 8, 1876), 370. One sign of the book's popularity was the publication of *Lyrics from "The Wide, Wide World"* (New York, 1853) with words by W. H. Bellamy (based on passages in *The Wide, Wide World*) and music by C. W. Glover. An advertisement of the day claimed, "In the 'Wide, Wide World' cannot be found better undergarments and hosiery than at James E. Ray's, 108 Bowery." (*Susan Warner*, p. 345.)

52. Hiram Haydn, *Words and Faces* (New York, 1974), p. 20.

53. Ibid., p. 20.

54. Carl Bode, *Antebellum Culture* (Carbondale, Ill., and Edwardsville, Ill., 1970), p. 176.

55. Helen Waite Papashvily, *All the Happy Endings* (New York, 1956), p. xvii.

56. *Susan Warner*, p. 293

57. Ibid., pp. 313, 305.

58. The plot of *The Wide, Wide World* is reminiscent, at least distantly, of Charlotte Brönte's *Jane Eyre* as well as *A New-England Tale*. All three books deal in part with orphans at the mercy of tyrannical aunts. It is worth noting that Susan closely identified with the heroine of the Brönte novel. Visiting with Mrs. David Codwise, she wrote home to her sister in April, 1848, "Mrs. Codwise has just run through Jane Eyre. Do you know she says I am so much like her, and wanted to know if you did not think so. I did not tell her that *I* thought so, but I do, as you know" (*Susan Warner*, p. 267). Susan was working on *The Wide, Wide World* when she wrote this letter, and one might assume that the character of Jane Eyre in part determined the character of Ellen Montgomery—but in fact the two characters are quite dissimilar. If the Brönte novel did influence Susan's work on *The Wide, Wide World*, the influence was distant and weak.

### Chapter Three

1. Susan Warner, "How May an American Woman Best Show Her Patriotism?" *"The Ladies' Wreath*, ed. Mrs. S. T. Martyn (New York, 1851), p. 317. This "essay" (actually a short story) was "A Prize Essay, which Received the Premium of Fifty Dollars"—the first payment which Susan received for her work.

2. Mrs. John Farrar, *the Young Lady's Friend* (Boston, 1838), p. 319.

3. Anna Warner, *Susan Warner ("Elizabeth Wetherell")* (New York, 1909), p. 295.

4. George Haven Putnam, *George Palmer Putnam: A Memoir* (New York, 1912), p. 295.

5. Ibid., p. 295.

6. *Susan Warner*, p. 281.

7. Ibid., p. 286.

8. Ibid., p. 319.

9. Ibid., p. 308.

10. Henry T. Tuckerman, "Biographical Essay," *Old New York: or, Reminisences of the Past Sixty Years* by John W. Francis (New York, 1865), p. lxxiv.

11. James D. McCabe, Jr., *Lights and Shadows of New York Life: or, the Sights and Sensations of the Great City* (New York, 1872), pp. 386 - 87.

12. Ibid., p. 386.

13. Alvin F. Harlow, *Old Bowery Days* (New York, 1931), p. 334.

14. A. A. Rikeman, *The Evolution of Stuyvesant Village* (Mamaroneck, N. Y.; 1899), p. 79.

15. Stow Persons, *The Decline of American Gentility* (New York, 1973), *passim.*

16. Farrar, *Young Lady's Friend*, p. 319.

17. Catharine Maria Sedgwick, *Morals of Manners* (New York, 1846), p. 4.

18. Persons, *Decline of American Gentility*, p. 37.

19. Farrar, *Young Lady's Friend*, p. 319.

20. Sedgwick, *Morals of Manners*, p. 22.

21. Susan Warner, *Queechy* (New York, 1852), I, 76.

22. Ibid., I, 96.

23. Ibid., I, 11.

24. Ibid., I, 117, 125.

25. Ibid., II, 155.

26. Ibid., II, 223 - 24.

27. Ibid., I, 194.

28. Ibid., I, 262.

29. Ibid., I, 226 - 27.

30. Ibid., I, 240.

31. Ibid., II, 72 - 73.

32. Portions of Chelsea were still fashionable, of course. The poet and classical scholar Clement Clarke Moore still lived here on the family estate, and there were several other elegant residences in the area, but already the southern portion of Chelsea had acquired that unsavory reputation that Fleda recognized.

33. *Queechy*, II, 49.

34. Ibid., I, 67.

35. Ibid., I, 285.

36. Anonymous, "American Novels," *North British Review*, XX (November, 1853), 101.

37. Edward G. Salmon, "What Girls Read," *The Nineteenth Century*, XX (October, 1886), 524.

38. Elizabeth Barrett Browning, *Letters*, ed. Frederick G. Kenyon, (New York, 1897), II, 134.

39. Anna Warner, *Dollars and Cents* (Philadelphia, 1888). The error is particularly striking since the plates used were those of the first edition. It seems most unlikely that the publisher did not know that the book was Anna's rather than Susan's—but he must also have known that a novel "BY THE AUTHOR OF THE WIDE WIDE WORLD" would attract more attention than a novel by the lesser known sister. The error, one suspects, was intentional.

40. Mabel Baker, *The Warner Family and the Warner Books* (West Point, N. Y.; 1971), pp. 9 - 10.

41. Bogert's will is filed at the Queens County (New York) Courthouse in Jamaica, Long Island. Bogert's early generosity to the Warners (particularly in connection with their land purchases in Brooklyn) and his social prestige were undoubtedly of enormous importance to Henry Whiting Warner's social and financial success. Why Bogert left the Warners out of his will is unknown, but he appears to have been disenchanted with the whole clan. His earlier generosity to his wife's family extended to her niece, Susan and Anna's cousin Sarah Helen Power, who lived for a time in Bogert's mansion on Long Island. Bogert also paid part of her educational expenses, and she returned and spent her honeymoon at his house. (After her marriage, she was known as Sarah Helen Whitman—the poet and friend of Edgar Allan Poe.) Clearly Bogert was most generous to his wife's niece during his lifetime, but neither she nor any of his wife's family benefited from his will. He left to his wife, in additon to a large yearly stipend, various articles of furniture and $4,000—a substantial sum at the time but a small fraction of his entire estate. Mrs. Bogert later lived with relatives, including Mrs. Whitman, in Providence, and there were apparently few contacts between her family and her husband's.

42. Susan Warner, *The Hills of the Shatemuc* (New York, 1856), p. 341.

43. Anonymous, review of *The Hills of the Shatemuc*, *The Athenaeum*, No. 1508 (September 20, 1856), 1163.

44. Ibid., p. 1164.

45. Charles Kingsley, *The Water-Babies* (London, 1903), p. 174.

## Chapter Four

1. Anna Warner, *Susan Warner ("Elizabeth Wetherell")* (New York, 1909), pp. 274 - 75.

2. "Jesus Loves Me" is, of course, one of the best-known hymns in the

English language and has even been recorded and successfully promoted as a popular song. It has had many notable defenders and supporters, including the great theologian Karl Barth, who is quoted as saying that the words were the most profound he had ever heard. (Robert F. Boyd, "The Integrity of the Bible," *The Presbyterian Journal,* XXXIV (September 17, 1975), 7.) According to John Hersey, John F. Kennedy joined his shipmates in singing the hymn during the rescue mission after his PT boat was destroyed in World War II. (Ardis Abbott, *Jesus Loves Me: Incidents from the Life of Anna Bartlett Warner* (West Point, N.Y.; 1967), p. 2.) The hymn begins,

> Jesus loves me, this I know,
> For the Bible tells me so:
> Little ones to Him belong.
> They are weak, but He is strong.
> Yes, Jesus loves me.
> Yes, Jesus loves me.
> Yes, Jesus loves me.
> The Bible tells me so.

3. The Stokes biography was commissioned by the family and privately published. It is, as one would expect, extremely reticent about the family's private life, but its account of their economic, social, and religious affairs is heavily detailed.

4. Olivia Egleston Phelps Stokes, *Letters and Memories of Susan and Anna Bartlett Warner* (New York, 1925), p. 6.

5. This fact was noted in an early introduction to the series but has generally been overlooked by biographers and critics.

6. Anna Warner, *Mr. Rutherford's Children* (New York, 1853), I, 145.

7. Anna Warner, *Dollars and Cents* (New York, 1852), I, 8.

8. Ibid., I, 9.

9. Ibid., I, 144.

10. Ibid., II, 346.

11. *Susan Warner,* p. 196.

12. Ibid., p. 198.

13. Ibid., p. 198.

14. Warner's financial affairs were complex, but surviving public records as well as scattered references in letters and journals allow us to piece together a general picture of his early economic success and subsequent bankruptcy. Warner dealt extensively in real estate in Brooklyn, but his largest investments were made in Manhattan. During his early married years—conceivably with advice and/or capital from Cornelius Bogert—he bought and sold various properties in New York; but between 1825 and 1833, there were no purchases. This may be attributable to the hugely inflated real-estate prices which accompanied the growth of the city immediately after the opening of the Erie Canal in 1825. Warner may not

have had sufficient funds to meet the new prices; or, since he was generally conservative in his speculations, he may have decided to wait until prices levelled off and showed no signs of fluctuating. In any case, between 1833 and 1836 he began investing in Manhattan real estate again—and he bought heavily: nine parcels in 1833, five in 1834, seventeen in 1835, seven in 1836. From time to time during these years, properties were sold—conceivably to provide funds for new and more lucrative investments.

The great depression of 1837 - 43 drove prices down—it was a good time to buy, but Warner now needed money to cover general expenses as well as mortgages. Between 1837 and 1841, he made only seven purchases, while at the same time he sold off nearly all of his remaining holdings. By the end of the depression, he owned little New York property.

1835 and 1836 were the best years for him financially. In these years he was able to purchase Constitution Island and the mansion on St. Mark's Place. As noted earlier, he intended to establish a summer estate for his family at Constitution Island, but he also planned to develop most of the acreage as a summer resort. The country's economic problems began during the spring of 1837, but Warner (who was already cautious about his real estate investments) brought Alexander Jackson Davis, the most famous American architect of the time, to the island to draw up plans for developing the place. For Warner, Davis produced drawings for an enormous Gothic hotel to be built at the water's edge. But the hotel did not materialize—nor did any of Warner's other plans for the island. To develop part of the island, it would have been necessary to build a dam and drain marshlands—but that dam was destroyed, as we have seen, and years of litigation followed, during which the marshlands remained. There were also difficulties with the terms of the mortgage, which resulted in further debts to pay and encumbrances upon the property which made it impossible to subdivide and sell sections.

In the late 1840s, the country was again in a state of economic difficulty; and Warner found himself again surrounded by financial problems, through, however, "a bit of chicanery" and no fault of his own (*Susan Warner*, p. 278). Most of the family's possessions went to meet the new debt—the law and the sheriff leaving the Warners with a few possessions, the farmhouse, and the island. Most of the furniture was gone, books and engravings as well. "Our little . . . front room was swept and dusted," Anna wrote, "stray bits of furniture were gathered in; and I ran out for a handful of flowers, to make myself feel at home" (Ibid., p. 279). This episode, like many others in the family's economic history, appears in *Dollars and Cents.*

15. *Dollars and Cents*, I, 50 - 51.
16. Ibid., I, 54 - 55.
17. Ibid., I, 55.
18. Ibid., II, 368.
19. Ibid., II, 368.

20. Anonymous, review of *My Brother's Keeper, Putnam's Monthly,* V (June, 1855), 661.

21. Ibid., p. 660.

22. Mabel Baker, *The Warner Family and the Warner Books* (West Point, N.Y.; 1971), p. 12.

23. *Susan Warner,* p. 407.

24. Anonymous, review of Say and Seal, The Athenaeum, No. 1692 (March 31, 1860), p. 441.

25. Susan and Anna Warner, *Say and Seal* (London, N.J.), p. 1.

26. I *Corinthians* XI.3. *Ephesians* V. 22 - 23.

27. *Say and Seal,* p. 406.

28. Ibid., p. 106.

29. Ibid., pp. 33 - 34.

30. Anonymous, review of *Say and Seal, Littell's Living Age,* IX (May, 1860), 410.

31. F. C. Hopkinson, review of *Say and Seal, Atlantic Monthly,* VI (July, 1860), 121.

32. Ibid., p. 121.

33. Ibid., p. 122.

## Chapter Five

1. Anna Warner, *Susan Warner ("Elizabeth Wetherell")* (New York, 1909), p. 376. It is curious that Anna says "repeats," for her sister at this time has been dead for nearly a quarter century.

2. A. C. C. [sic], *Robert Carter: His Life and Work: 1807 - 1889* (New York, 1891), p. 87.

3. Ibid., p. 86.

4. Susan and Anna's principal English publisher was James Nesbit. Nesbit was as adamantly evangelical in his religious persuasions as were the Warners and Carter. Nesbit's biography, *Lessons from the Life of James Nesbit, the Publisher,* written by his son-in-law, is an excellent example of evangelical didacticism. Henry Curwen in *A History of Booksellers* (London, 1873) noted that the book is not " 'a mere biography'—would that it were!—but a series of forty chapters or lessons, each commencing with a text and ending with a hymn" (p. 325). It was certainly the sort of biography of which the Warners would have approved.

5. Susan Warner, *Pine Needles* (New York, 1877), p. 129.

6. *Susan Warner,* p. 456.

7. Susan Warner, *Walks from Eden* (New York, 1865), p. iii.

8. Ibid., p. iii.

9. *Susan Warner,* p. 456.

10. Anonymous, "A Religious Novel," *Blackwood's Edinburgh Magazine,* XCIX (March, 1866), 275 - 86.

11. Anonymous, "More Children's Books," *The Nation*, IX (December 23, 1869), 568.

12. Ibid., p. 568.

13. *Susan Warner*, p. 403.

14. Ibid., p. 408.

15. Ibid., p. 416.

16. Henry Whiting Warner, *Fifty Years Progress* (Albany, N.Y.; 1859), p. 10.

17. Ibid., p. 17.

18. Ibid., p. 17.

19. Ibid., p. 17.

20. Susan and Anna Warner, *The Gold of Chickaree* (New York, 1876), p. 420.

21. Ibid., p. 421.

22. Ibid., p. 421.

23. Ibid., p. 422.

24. Ibid., p. 421.

25. Susan and Anna Warner, *Wych Hazel* (New York, 1876), pp. 32 - 33.

26. Ibid., p. 100.

27. Ibid., p. 102.

28. A. W. H. [sic], review of *Wych Hazel, The Library Table*, I (June, 1876), 78.

29. Anonymous, review of *Wych Hazel, Appleton's Journal*, XV (June 3, 1876), 130.

30. Ibid., p. 131.

31. Anonymous, review of *Wych Hazel, Atlantic Monthly*, XXXVIII (September, 1876), 368.

32. Anonymous, review of *The Gold of Chickaree, Atlantic Monthly*, XXXIX (March, 1877).

33. Anonymous, review of *The Gold of Chickaree, The Nation*, XXIV (May 10, 1877), p. 282.

### Chapter Six

1. Susan Warner, *Daisy Plains* (New York, 1885), p. 85.

2. Susan Warner, *My Desire* (New York, 1879), p. 5.

3. Susan Warner, *Diana* (New York, 1877), p. 1. *Diana* was published by G. P. Putnam's Sons, but all of the other "factual" novels were issued by Carter.

4. Anonymous, review of *Nobody, The Nation*, XXXV (November 23, 1882), 448.

5. Susan Warner, *Stephen, M. D.* (New York, 1883), p. 22.

6. *Daisy Plains*, p. 608.

7. Susan Warner, *The Letter of Credit* (New York, 1881), p. 122.

### Chapter Seven

1. Anna Warner, *Susan Warner ("Elizabeth Wetherell")* (New York, 1909), p. 477.

2. Ibid., p. 2.

3. Ibid., p. 3.

4. See, for example, his comments on the subject which are quoted above, p. 97.

5. Caroline Kirkland, review of *The Wide, Wide World, Queechy,* and *Dollars and Cents; The North American Review,* LXXVI (January, 1853), 112, 122.

6. Ibid., p. 105.

7. Ibid., p. 111.

8. Ibid., p. 114.

9. Ibid., pp. 120, 115 - 16.

10. Ibid., p. 122.

11. Ibid., p. 122.

12. Ibid., p. 122.

13. Susan Warner, "How May an American Woman Best Show Her Patriotism?" *The Ladies Wreath,* ed. Mrs. S. T. Martyn (New York, 1851), p. 326.

14. Thomas Wentworth Higginson, *Women and Men* (New York, 1887), p. 289.

15. Ibid., p. 289.

16. Of Miss Sedgwick, Higginson wrote, "A greater loss to memory is the fame of Miss Sedgwick, whose graphic and sensible fiction—realistic in the best sense—seems absolutely unknown to the generation now growing up." (Ibid., p. 289) A few decades later, the same could have been said of Susan Warner.

# Selected Bibliography

PRIMARY SOURCES

1. Works by Anna Warner
*A Bag of Stories*. R. Carter and Brothers, 1883
*Blue Flag and Cloth of Gold*. R. Carter and Brothers, 1879.
*Casper*. New York: G. P. Putnam and Co., 1856.
*Cross Corners*. New York: R. Carter and Brothers, 1887.
*Dollars and Cents*. New York: G. P. Putnam, 1852.
*The Fourth Watch*. New York: A. D. F. Randolph and Co., c. 1872.
*Fresh Air*. New York: American Tract Society, c. 1899.
*Gardening by Myself*. New York: A. D. F. Randolph and Co., 1872.
*Hard Maple*. Boston: Shepard, Clark and Brown, 1859.
*Hymns of the Church Militant*. New York: R. Carter and Brothers, 1858.
*Little Jack's Four Lessons*. New York: R. Carter and Brothers, 1869.
*The Light of the Morning*. New York: A. D. F. Randolph, 1882.
*The Melody of the Twenty-Third Psalm*. New York: A. D. F. Randolph and Co.; 1869.
*Miss Muff and Little Hungry*. Philadelphia: Presbyterian Publication Committee, c. 1866.
*Miss Tiller's Vegetable Garden and the Money She Made by It*. New York: A. D. F. Randolph and Co., 1872.
*Mr. Rutherford's Children*. New York: G. P. Putnam, 1853.
*Mr. Rutherford's Children* (second volume). New York: G. P. Putnam, 1854.
*My Brother's Keeper*. New York: D. Appleton and Co., 1855.
*The Other Shore*. New York: A. D. F. Randolph, 1872.
*Patience*. Philadelphia: J. B. Lippincott Co., 1890.
*Robinson Crusoe's Farmyard*. New York: G. P. Putnam, 1848.
*A Servant of the King, Incidents in the Life of Rev. George Ainslie*. New York: J. Ireland, 1889.
*The Shoes of Peace*. New York: R. Carter and Brothers, 1884.
*Some Memories of James Stokes and Caroline Phelps Stokes*. Cambridge, Mass.: H. O. Houghton, 1892.
*The Star out of Jacob*. New York: R. Carter and Brothers, 1866.
Stories of Vinegar Hill. New York: R. Carter and Brothers, 1866. A series of volumes including *The Old Church Door, The Fowls of the Air, Golden Thorns, Plants without Root, An Hundredfold, Spring Work*.

*Susan Warner ("Elizabeth Wetherell").* New York: G. P. Putnam's Sons, 1909.

*Three Little Spades.* New York: Harper and Brothers, 1868.

*Tired Church Members.* New York: R. Carter and Brothers, 1881.

*Up and Down the House.* New York: A. D. F. Randolph and Co., c. 1892.

*Wayfaring Hymns, Original and Translated.* New York: A. D. F. Randolph and Co., 1869.

*West Point Colors.* New York: F. H. Revell, 1903.

*What Aileth Thee.* New York: A. D. F. Randolph and Co., 1880.

*Yours and Mine.* New York: R. Carter and Brothers, 1888.


## 2. Works by Susan Warner

*American Female Patriotism.* N. p.: E. H. Fletcher, 1852. Originally published as "How May an American Woman Best Show Her Patriotism?" *The Ladies' Wreath: An Illustrated Annual.* New York: J. M. Fletcher and Co., 1851.

*Bread and Oranges.* New York: R. Carter and Brothers, 1875.

*The Broken Walls of Jerusalem and the Rebuilding of Them.* New York: R. Carter and Brothers, 1870.

*Carl Krinken: His Christmas Stocking.* New York: G. P. Putnam, 1853.

*Daisy.* Philadelphia: J. B. Lippincott and Co., 1868.

*Daisy, Second Series.* Philadelphia: J. B. Lippincott and Co., 1869.

*Daisy Plains.* New York: R. Carter and Brothers, 1885.

*Diana.* New York: G. P. Putnam's Sons, 1877.

*The End of a Coil.* New York: R. Carter and Brothers, 1880.

*The Flag of Truce.* New York: R. Carter and Brothers, 1875.

*The Hills of the Shatemuc.* New York: D. Appleton and Co., 1856.

*The House in Town.* New York: R. Carter and Brothers, 1870.

*The House of Israel.* New York: R. Carter and Brothers, 1866.

*The Kingdom of Judah.* R. Carter and Brothers, 1878.

*The Law and the Testimony.* New York: R. Carter and Brothers, 1853.

*Lessons on the Standard Bearers of the Old Testament.* New York: A. D. F. Randolph, 1872.

*The Letter of Credit.* New York: R. Carter and Brothers, 1881.

*The Little Camp on Eagle Hill.* New York: R. Carter and Brothers, 1873.

*The Little Nurse of Cape Cod.* Philadelphia: American Sunday-School Union, c. 1863.

*Melbourne House.* New York: Robert Carter and Brothers, 1864.

*My Desire.* New York: R. Carter and Brothers, 1879.

*Nobody.* New York: R. Carter and Brothers, 1882.

*The Old Helmet.* New York: R. Carter and Brothers, 1863.

*Opportunities.* New York: R. Carter and Brothers, 1870.

*Pine Needles.* New York: R. Carter and Brothers, 1877.

*Queechy.* New York: G. P. Putnam, 1852.

*The Rapids of Niagara.* New York: R. Carter and Brothers, 1876.
*A Red Wallflower.* New York: R. Carter and Brothers, 1884.
*Sceptres and Crowns.* New York: R. Carter and Brothers, 1874.
*Stephen, M. D.* New York: R. Carter and Brothers, 1883.
*Trading.* New York: R. Carter and Brothers, 1872.
*Walks from Eden.* New York: R. Carter and Brothers, 1865.
*"What She Could".* New York: R. Carter and Brothers, 1870.
*The Wide, Wide World.* New York: G. P. Putnam, 1850.
*Willow Brook.* R. Carter and Brothers, 1874.

3. Works by Susan and Anna Warner
*The Gold of Chickaree.* New York: G. P. Putnam's Sons, 1876.
*The Little American.* New York: 1862 - 64. A magazine for children edited
    by the Warners. Two volumes, twenty-two issues.
*Martha's Hymn.* New York: Carleton and Porter, 1862.
*The Rose in the Desert.* New York: R. Carter and Brothers, 1864.
*Say and Seal.* Philadelphia: J. B. Lippincott Co., 1860.
*Wych Hazel.* New York: G. P. Putnam's Sons, 1876.

4. *Works by Henry Whiting Warner*
*A Discourse on Legal Science.* New York: G. and C. and H. Carvill, 1833.
*Fifty Years Progress.* Albany, N. Y.: Weed, Parsons, and Co., 1859.
*An Inquiry into the Moral and Religious Character of the American
    Government.* New York: Wiley and Putnam, 1838.
*The Liberties of America.* New York: G. P. Putnam and Co., 1853.
*An Oration . . . in Commemoration of the Nativity of George Washington.*
    New York: B. Gardenier, 1814.
Warner also transcribed and published the proceedings of the trial of C. N.
    Baldwin in 1818; prepared the American edition of Clement Tudway
    Swanston's *Chancery Reports*; and prepared the American edition of
    John Beanes's *A Brief Review of the Writ Ne Exeat Regno, with Prac-
    tical Remarks upon It as an Equitable Process.*

SECONDARY SOURCES

*Bibliographical*
ANONYMOUS. "Bibliography of the Works of Susan Warner and Anna
    Bartlett Warner," *Fourth Report and Year Book* of the Martelaer's
    Rock Association. Highland Falls, N. Y.: Book Hill Press, 1923. Can be
    misleading, since the author fails to note, for example, that *Dollars and
    Cents; Glen Luna, or Dollars and Cents; Grace Howard, and the
    Family at Glen Luna; Speculation; or, the Glen Luna Family*, and *The
    Glen Luna Family*—all of which are given separate entries—are in
    fact the same book. There are several problems of this nature; but for

more than fifty years, this was the only bibliography available, and
critics and biographers have used it extensively if not always
profitably.

SANDERSON, DOROTHY HURLBUT. *They Wrote for a Living*. West Point,
N.Y.: Constitution Island Association, 1976. A superb bibliography
which should be consulted by all future scholars interested in the
Warners.

*Critical and Biographical Studies*

ABBOTT, ARDIS, comp. *Jesus Loves Me: Incidents from the Life of Anna
Bartlett Warner*. West Point, N. Y.: Constitution Island Association,
1967. A brief survey of Anna's life and works, especially "Jesus Loves
Me." her most famous hymn.

BAKER, MABEL. *The Warner Family and the Warner Books*. West Point, N.
Y.: Constitution Island Association, 1971. A valuable general survey
which suggests various parallels between the Warners' lives and their
fiction.

BODE, CARL. *The Anatomy of American Popular Culture, 1840 - 1861*.
Berkeley and Los Angeles: The Univ. of California Press, 1960.
Reprinted as *Antebellum Culture*. Carbondale, Ill., and Edwardsville,
Ill.; Southern Illinois University Press, 1969. Examines *The Wide,
Wide World* in terms of Jungian archetypes.

COWIE, ALEXANDER. *The Rise of the American Novel*. New York; American
Book Co., 1951. Includes the standard survey of the domestic novel.

D_____, F. S. [sic] "Tears, Idle Tears." *The Critic*, XXI (October 29,
1892), 236 - 37. An amusing article on Ellen Montgomery's penchant
for tears.

DENMAN, FRANK. "How to Drive the Sheriff from Your Door." *The New
York Times Book Review*, Dec. 24, 1944, p. 8. An amusing but superficial study of *The Wide, Wide World*, a novel "in which the curious
preoccupations and evasions of the Victorian mind reach full flower."

FOSTER, EDWARD HALSEY. *The Civilized Wilderness: Backgrounds to
American Romantic Literature, 1817 - 1860*. New York; Free Press,
1975. Analyzes *The Wide, Wide World* within the context of
nineteenth-century American idealization of domesticity.

JORDAN, ALICE M. "Susan Warner and Her Wide, Wide World." *The Horn
Book*, X (September, 1934), 287 - 93. Examines *the Wide, Wide World*
as a book for girls and as "the first important example of the Sunday
School book type." The essay is reprinted in Jordan's *From Rollo to
Tom Sawyer* (Boston: Horn Book, 1948).

[KIRKLAND, CAROLINE]. Review of *The Wide, Wide World, Queechy*, and
*Dollars and Cents. The North American Review*, LXXVI (January,
1853), 104 - 23. An important review by one of the Warners' contemporaries. Examines the novels as expressions of the American
character.

LOCHHEAD, MARION. "Stars and Striplings: American Youth in the Nineteenth Century." *Quarterly Review*, V (April, 1959), 180 - 88. Studies Susan Warner's childhood in view of nineteenth-century American attitudes toward childhood.

MOTT, FRANK LUTHER. *Golden Multitudes: The Story of the Best Sellers in the United States*. New York: Macmillan, 1947. Representative example of the ungenerous critical attitude toward Susan Warner that prevailed in the middle years of this century.

OVERMYER, GRACE. "Hudson River Bluestockings — The Warner Sisters of Constitution Island." *New York History*, XL (April, 1959), 137 - 58. Well researched study of the Warners' lives.

PAPASHVILY, HELEN WAITE. *All the Happy Endings*. New York: Harper and Row, 1956. A standard work interpreting domestic novels from a feminist perspective. Places *The Wide, Wide World* and *Queechy* at the head of the tradition of the domestic novel.

PUTNAM, GEORGE HAVEN. "The Warner Sisters and the Literary Associations of the Hudson River Valley." *Fourth Report and Year Book of the Martelaer's Rock Association*. Highland Falls, N. Y.: Book Hill Press, 1923. Personal reminiscences of the Warners together with an examination of their works in the context of other works by writers who lived in, or wrote about, the Hudson River valley and vicinity.

REYNOLDS, CUYLER. "The Author of 'The Wide, Wide World.'" *The National Magazine*, IX (October, 1898), 73 - 81. Discusses Susan's use of Canaan settings in her novels.

SMITH, HENRY NASH. "The Scribbling Women and the Cosmic Success Story." *Critical Inquiry*, I (September, 1974), 47 - 70. A major contribution to American cultural history; deals essentially with the conformist attitudes of *The Wide, Wide World* and other popular mid-nineteenth-century American novels.

STOKES, MRS. ANSON PHELPS, and others. *Recollections of Miss Susan and Miss Anna Warner*. N. p.: Constitution Island Association, n. d. A collection of essays from the yearbooks of the Constitution Island Association. Includes "Personal Recollections of the Misses Warner" by Mrs. Anson Phelps Stokes; "The Author of *The Wide, Wide World*" by Christine Starr; "The One Hundredth Anniversary of *the Wide, Wide World*" by Colonel Girard L. McEntree; and "Glimpses of a Quiet Life Revealed in Bundle of Old Letters" (letters from the Warner sisters to their cousin, Mrs. Sarah Helen Whitman).

STOKES, OLIVIA E. PHELPS. *Letters and Memories of Susan and Anna Bartlett Warner*. New York: G. P. Putnam's Sons, 1925. An important compilation of letters and biographical anecdotes together with a genealogical record (incomplete, however) of the Warner family.

WARNER, ANNA. *Susan Warner ("Elizabeth Wetherell")*. New York: G. P. Putnam's Sons, 1909. This is the standard biography and a rich mine of biographical information. Written by an adoring sister and never critical of either its subject or the novels and other writings, it is, non-etheless, astonishingly frank in details of Susan's private life and her family's economic problems. Quotes freely from private letters and journals. Heavily documents the overlap between literary and religious worlds in nineteenth-century America.

# Index

135

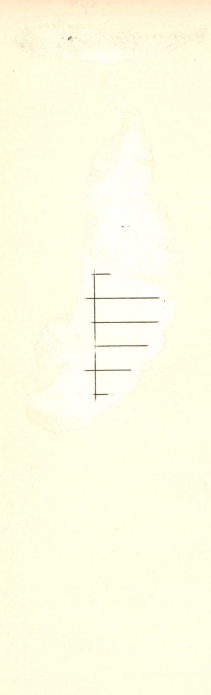